# Philosophical Perspectives on Religious Diversity

Addressing the question of what kind of theoretical foundations are required if we wish to have a constructive attitude towards different religions, this book scrutinizes aspects of the human condition, personhood and notions of (exclusive) truth and tolerance.

In the book, Wolterstorff suggests that persons have hermeneutic and related competences that account for their special dignity, and that this dignity implies the right to practice religion freely. Margolis emphasizes the contingent character of all religious pursuits – being products of a unique form of evolution, humans need to create convincing purposes in an otherwise purposeless world. Respondents criticize both views with an eye on the question of whether those views promote religious tolerance.

Grube criticizes the tendency for interreligious dialogue to be pursued under the parameters of an exclusive, bivalent notion of truth according to which something is necessarily false if it is not true. Under those parameters, religions that differ from the (one) true religion must be false. This explains why religious pluralists attempt to minimize the differences between religions at all costs and why others suggest implausibly strong concepts of tolerance. As an alternative, Grube proposes to drop exclusive concepts of truth and to conduct the interreligious dialogue under the parameters of the concept of justification which allows for pluralisation. The following discussion takes up this criticism of bivalence and its consequences for dealing with religious otherness.

This book was originally published as a special issue of the *International Journal of Philosophy and Theology*.

**Dirk-Martin Grube** holds the chair in Religious Diversity and the Epistemology of Theology/Religion at the Vrije Universiteit Amsterdam, The Netherlands.

**Walter Van Herck** is Associate Professor of Philosophy of Religion at the University of Antwerp, Belgium. He is editor-in-chief of the *International Journal of Philosophy and Theology*.

# Philosophical Perspectives on Religious Diversity

Bivalent Truth, Tolerance and Personhood

*Edited by*
**Dirk-Martin Grube and Walter Van Herck**

LONDON AND NEW YORK

First published 2018
by Routledge

2 Park Square, Milton Park, Abingdon, Oxfordshire OX14 4RN
52 Vanderbilt Avenue, New York, NY 10017

*Routledge is an imprint of the Taylor & Francis Group, an informa business*

First issued in paperback 2019

*British Library Cataloguing in Publication Data*
A catalogue record for this book is available from the British Library

ISBN 13: 978-1-138-10462-4 (hbk)
ISBN 13: 978-0-367-89111-4 (pbk)

Typeset in Times New Roman
by RefineCatch Limited, Bungay, Suffolk

**Publisher's Note**
The publisher accepts responsibility for any inconsistencies that may have
arisen during the conversion of this book from journal articles to book chapters,
namely the possible inclusion of journal terminology.

**Disclaimer**
Every effort has been made to contact copyright holders for their permission to
reprint material in this book. The publishers would be grateful to hear from any
copyright holder who is not here acknowledged and will undertake to rectify
any errors or omissions in future editions of this book.

# Contents

CONTENTS

# Citation Information

The chapters in this book were originally published in the *International Journal of Philosophy and Theology*, volume 76, issue 5 (December 2015). When citing this material, please use the original page numbering for each article, as follows:

For any permission-related enquiries please visit:
http://www.tandfonline.com/page/help/permissions

# Notes on Contributors

**Christoph Baumgartner** is Associate Professor of Ethics at the Department of Philosophy and Religious Studies at Utrecht University, The Netherlands. Principal topics of his research include religion in the public sphere, freedom of religion and freedom of expression, secularism and (post)secularity, citizenship in religiously pluralistic societies, freedom of religion and children, environmental ethics, and intergenerational justice.

**Vincent Brümmer** was Professor of Philosophy of Religion at Utrecht University, The Netherlands, from 1967 to 1997. His books include *What Are We Doing When We Pray?* (1984, revised and expanded Ashgate, 2008) and *Contemporary Thinkers on Religion. Brümmer on Meaning and the Christian Faith. Collected Writings of Vincent Brümmer* (Ashgate, 2006).

**Dirk-Martin Grube** holds the chair in Religious Diversity and the Epistemology of Theology/Religion at the Vrije Universiteit Amsterdam, The Netherlands. He has published monographs on Paul Tillich, Christology, interpretation theory, pragmatism, contingency and the foundation of (Christian) ethics as well as articles on the intersection between philosophy (of religion) and theology.

**Peter Jonkers** is Professor of Philosophy at the School of Catholic Theology, Tilburg University, The Netherlands. He teaches systematic philosophy, contemporary continental philosophy, metaphysics, and philosophy of culture. His current research interests include religious truth in a pluralist society, the relation between truth and wisdom, tolerance, and Hegel and his contemporaries.

**Joseph Margolis** is currently Laura H. Carnell Professor of Philosophy at Temple University, Philadelphia, PA, USA. His main interests are in the philosophy of the human sciences, the theory of knowledge and interpretation, aesthetics, philosophy of mind, American philosophy, and pragmatism.

**Sami Pihlström** is Professor of Philosophy of Religion at the University of Helsinki, Finland. His recent books include *Transcendental Guilt: Reflections on Ethical Finitude* (2011), *Pragmatic Pluralism and the Problem of God* (2013), *Taking Evil Seriously* (2014), and *The Bloomsbury Companion to Pragmatism* (2011).

**Nicola Slee** is Director of Research at the Queen's Foundation for Ecumenical Theological Education, Birmingham, UK. She has wide-ranging interests and publications in the intersections between feminism, faith, liturgy, spirituality, and poetry. Her publications include *The Faith Lives of Women and Girls: Qualitative Research Perspectives* (co-edited with Porter and Phillips, Ashgate, 2013) and *Making Nothing Happen: Five Poets Explore Spirituality* (with D'Costa, Nesbitt, Pryce and Shelton, Ashgate 2014).

**Luco J. van den Brom** is Extraordinary Professor of Systematic Theology at the University of Pretoria, South Africa. He is also Professor Emeritus of Systematic Theology at the Dutch Protestant Theological University Groningen, and Professor Emeritus of Philosophical Theology at the University of Groningen. He publishes on philosophical and doctrinal theology, on science and religion, and fundamental theology.

**Walter Van Herck** is Associate Professor of Philosophy of Religion at the University of Antwerp, Belgium. He is editor-in-chief of the *International Journal of Philosophy and Theology*.

**René van Woudenberg** is Professor of Philosophy at the Vrije Universiteit, Amsterdam, The Netherlands, where he teaches Epistemology and Metaphysics. He is the Director of the Abraham Kuyper Center for Science and Religion.

**Oliver J. Wiertz** is Professor of Philosophy at Sankt Georgen Graduate School for Philosophy and Theology, Frankfurt/Main, Germany. His research focuses on epistemology and analytic philosophy of religion. He has published articles on the rationality of religious faith, the theistic concept of God, the problem of evil, religious plurality, and religious violence.

**Maarten Wisse** is Professor of Systematic Theology at the Protestant Theological University, Amsterdam, The Netherlands, and Privatdozent in Systematic Theology at the Eberhard Karls University, Tübingen, Germany.

**Nicholas Wolterstorff** is Emeritus Professor of Philosophical Theology, Yale University, USA. He is currently a Senior Fellow at the Institute for Advanced Studies in Culture at the University of Virginia, USA.

# Introduction

This special edition of the *International Journal of Philosophy and Theology* emerges out of a conference at the Vrije Universiteit Amsterdam on 24 September 2015, entitled 'Religious Diversity: Philosophical Perspectives.'

The urgency of the topic needs hardly any explanation: In Europe and elsewhere, we are faced with a diversity of different religions which occupy the same public space. We thus have to come to terms with this diversity one way or the other. If we wish to come to terms with it in a responsible fashion, we need to reflect on it in a serious way. This special edition focuses on the *philosophical* reflection on the issue. Its purpose is to add to the existing discourses a 'theoretical-foundational' reflection, a *Grundlagenreflexion* on religious diversity. Such a reflection is highly necessary in a situation in which the discussion on the issue is highly polarized – in the political realm but also in the philosophical one[1] – and catchphrases are widespread. This reflection attempts to provide a responsible philosophical analysis of the possibility of accepting religious diversity and the opportunities and challenges it provides. Hopefully, it will trigger further discussion and provide a useful basis for moral and, eventually, political decision-making on this crucial issue.

Three main papers were given at the conference, by *Nicholas Wolterstorff*, *Joseph Margolis* and myself (my inaugural lecture). *Christoph Baumgartner* and *Maarten Wisse* responded to Wolterstorff's paper, and *Oliver Wiertz* and *Nicola Slee* to Margolis's paper. *René* van *Woudenberg*, *Vincent Brümmer*, *Sami Pihlström*, *Peter Jonkers* and *Luco van den Brom* responded to my inaugural lecture after the conference. All those papers and responses, plus my *Concluding Remarks* are collected in this special edition.

*Wolterstorff* targets the issue of toleration. He emphasizes that we should distinguish between toleration and indifference. He argues that '[i]ndifference makes toleration irrelevant', genuine toleration requires caring about the issue at stake and, also, disapproving of it. After providing some historical considerations on the issue, he emphasizes that being a human person implies *hermeneutic* capacities, i.e. the capacity to *interpret* reality, and to have a 'valorized identity,' i.e. the capacity to form judgments on the relative importance a 'person assigns to states and events in her life'. Both hermeneutic and valorizing capacities account, among others, for the special dignity of persons. That being the case, persons have 'a natural right' to be treated in ways that befit their dignity which includes 'the civil right to free exercise of their religions'.

*Baumgartner* criticizes that Wolterstorff runs the notions of religious toleration and that of the right to freedom of religion together: The latter appears illegitimately to be a subspecies of the former. Furthermore, Baumgartner argues that Wolterstorff bases the special dignity on capacities of human persons, not of human beings in general so that his account of freedom of religion is not a *human* right but one of persons.

The counter-question to Baumgartner is to what extent Wolterstorff's argument requires reference to human rights: Could the emphasis upon toleration and the free exercise of religion not be had without reference to the notion of human rights and be consistently reconstructed as a 'dignity of persons' – argument?

*Wisse* emphasizes that the grounds for toleration of other religions than the home-religion should be *religious* rather than philosophical: 'Motivations for religious tolerance are intrinsically contextual and relative to one's religious tradition ...'. Pointing out that Christianity is *itself* a product of an intra- and interreligious dialogue, he emphasizes the need for religious tolerance and dialogue. Providing the example of a concern for the good life, Wisse insists that both Buddhists and Christians share common ground. Yet, in accord with what a number of other contributors emphasize (e.g. Wolterstorff and myself), Wisse rejects the view that the search for common ground is the purpose of the inter-religious dialogue. Rather, it is an 'invitation to discover what God has given in other religions through creation and revelation ...'.

The counter-question to Wisse is whether an emphasis upon the theological roots of tolerance needs to be played off that strongly against the search for a philosophical basis of it. Aren't both more compatible than Wisse thinks? Is the philosophical search not a meta-endeavour which provides the fundamental-theoretical foundations for the *possibility* of tolerance – without which the theological endeavours would be pointless?

*Margolis* emphasizes the contingent character of all religious pursuits: There are no such things as timeless truths regarding religion.[2] *Homo sapiens* does not occupy any determinate ecological niche or teleological function in terms of which the objectives of religion could be discovered. Yet, Margolis holds that persons are '*hybrid artifacts* of a unique form of evolution peculiar to the human species, creatures that, by mastering language [and self-reflectivity], are effectively capacitated to invent encompassing objectives for their own lives' (emphasis added). In order to survive, they need 'steady, convincing purposes in a purposeless world' and religion is an important source of providing such purposes. Yet, the logic driving such 'invented rather than discovered' purposes requires us to retreat from a bivalent notion of truth to a many-valued notion or, as Margolis calls it here, a 'relativistic logic' (for the issue of retreating from bivalence, see also later).

*Wiertz* summarizes Margolis' account as implying that every religion has to acknowledge its deeply historical and contingent character: There are no neutral grounds but justifications are internal to the religion at stake. Wiertz emphasizes that, for Margolis, human beings are artefactual persons who have to construct themselves as well as their norms and purposes. But Wiertz suggests that *that* is precisely what makes them special: Human beings are the only species which is in a position to create itself, to develop a 'language sufficient for discursive aims'. Wiertz embeds this suggestion in a classical metaphysics.

The counter-question to raise to Wiertz is whether the difference between his anthropological presuppositions and Margolis' are as huge as Wiertz seems to assume. Although this comes out in his paper only marginally, Margolis is in the records for criticizing the 'profound inadequacy of the Darwinian model of evolution' by drawing on post-Darwinian palaeoanthropology. According to Margolis, the human species is 'biologically formed to be *cultural* animals',[3] and language, intentionality and (self-)consciousness emerge within the bounds of the natural but cannot be nomologically inferred from it in the sense in which materialists attempt to do so. Although Margolis will reject Wiertz's emphasis upon a classical metaphysics, the idea that the human species is unique for its use of lingual capabilities is not at all foreign to Margolis.

Being a practical and feminist theologian, *Slee* emphasizes the need to root the philosophical discourse on religious diversity within the lived experience (of women) of faith. Her main point is not so much to reject Margolis' approach but to question some of the standard assumptions Margolis and others make (in Slee's eyes) when talking about religious diversity. Referring to her own experiences, e.g. with an interfaith group of women in Birmingham, Slee suggests that differences between deviant religious traditions may be relativized by the shared experience of marginalization. Rather than religious differences, differences in power, status, ethnicity, etc. may be at the foreground of the agenda. Her conclusion is that what we see to be key differences in the discourse on religious diversity 'will depend to a large extent on our context, social location and agenda' so that our 'experiences of difference will also keep shifting'.

The counter-question to Slee is whether the theoretical reflection on religious differences must be played off that strongly against the 'lived experience' of (religious) difference. Obviously, Slee's insistence on the situatedness of our perceptions of difference is a useful warning against all tendencies to 'essentialize' them. And insisting on the contrast between theory and practice is valuable when deconstructing the (traditional) tendency to overemphasize theory over practice. Yet, is such a stark contrast also helpful when it comes to *reconstructing* the discourse on religious diversity in a responsible fashion? Is it for the purposes of such a reconstruction not more helpful to think along the lines of a *continuum between theory and praxis*, a mutual interaction according to which one influences the other without principally privileging theory or practice?

In my *inaugural lecture*, I criticize religious pluralist approaches, such as *John Hick's*, and their attempts to find common ground between the different religions at all costs. They are guided by the assumption that that which is different must be false. I trace this assumption back to bivalent presuppositions and reject a bivalent logic with its exclusive alternative 'either true or false'. I suggest to drop the notion of truth and use that of justification in order to distinguish between epistemically praiseworthy and epistemically blameworthy behaviour. Furthermore, I suggest that justification is context-dependent and thus pluralizable in a way in which truth is not. The pluralization of justification is the key to dealing constructively with the issue of religious diversity in my view: Religious believers in different contexts can be justified to hold different religious beliefs. This is the *core of the paradigm of justified religious difference*. This paradigm implies a number of consequences for reconstructing the interreligious dialogue. One of them is that the desperate search for common ground should be abandoned in favour of acknowledging genuine differences between the religions.

My criticism of bivalence is rejected by *van Woudenberg, Brümmer* and *Pihlström*: According to van Woudenberg, most religious believers accept bivalence and abandoning it would licence 'madness'. Brümmer insists that bivalence, respectively, 'excluded middle' (i.e. that *either* a proposition *or* its negation is true) is a necessary condition for 'the success of any legitimate speech act.' *Pihlström* suggests to pay close attention to where bivalence applies and where it does not. He suggests to endorse a general fallibilism rather than a rejection of bivalence.

Following Ricoeur, *Jonkers* advocates a very strong notion of tolerance which he plays off against my account: He suggests that we should not only tolerate what we consider to be justified but also that which we consider to be *unjustified*. *Van den Brom* emphasizes the difference between religious beliefs and knowledge claims. According to him, the issue of the justification of deviant religious beliefs can be dealt with only from *within* the parameters of particular religious inside-perspectives.

In my *Concluding Remarks*, I respond to the issues my critics have raised: After pondering on the reasons why I consider a (broadly) semantic notion of truth to be crucial (Sections 1–2), I explain what I mean by the notions of 'bivalence' and '*tertium non datur*' (3) and respond to *van Woudenberg's, Brümmer's and Pihlström's* criticism (4). But I admit that nothing much hangs on deconstructing those notions. The real issue is that of an *exclusivist competition*, viz. that belief A necessarily displaces the deviant belief B (5). We need to abrogate *this kind of displacement relation* in the discourse on religious diversity as well as in many other academic and cultural discourses (as I demonstrate with the help of a criticism of Dawkins' atheism) (6).

I explain why I consider the traditional concept of tolerance to be less important than my critics assume (7) and criticize *Jonkers'* strong notion of tolerance (8). After specifying why I think that justification can be pluralized and that this is the key to the 'justified difference' approach I favour (9), I respond to the challenges *Pihlström, van den Brom*, and *van Woudenberg* raise regarding my use of the notion of justification (10). Finally, I provide a sketch of the *theory of 'justified difference'* I have in mind, drawing on the distinction between disagreement with a deviant belief which is false and disagreement with a deviant belief which is not false (11).

## Notes

1. Recently, a number of Dutch philosophers signed a petition in which they plead that Europeans should be (more) 'open' to migrants ('Wij zijn allemaal migranten', Marli Huijer et al., published in Trouw, 30 March 2016, 'De Verdieping', 8).
2. It should be noted, though, that Margolis would be prepared to hold that there do not exist time-less truths in other disciplines as well, including (natural) scientific disciplines (see, e.g., Margolis, *Texts without Referents*).
3. (Emphasis mine). All quotes from Grube, "Introduction," xii (see also below, my Concluding Remarks, f. 4).

## Bibliography

Grube, D.-M. "Introduction." In *Pragmatism, Metaphysics and Culture. Reflections on the Philosophy of Joseph Margolis*, edited by D. M. Grube and R. Sinclair, vi–xxvi. Helsinki, 2015. http://www.nordprag.org/nsp/2/Introduction.pdf.

Margolis, J. *Texts without Referents. Reconciling Science and Narrative*. Oxford: Blackwell, 1989.

Dirk-Martin Grube

# Toleration, justice, and dignity. Lecture on the occasion of the inauguration as professor of Dirk-Martin Grube, Free University of Amsterdam, September 24, 2015

Nicholas Wolterstorff

After discussing the nature of toleration, giving a brief history of the emergence of religious toleration in the West, and presenting my understanding of religion, I develop what I call 'the dignity argument' for religious toleration: to fail to tolerate a person's religion is to treat that person in a way that does not befit their dignity. And to treat them in a way that does not befit their dignity is to wrong them, to treat them unjustly.

Before I begin my discussion, let me warmly congratulate Dirk-Martin Grube on his inauguration as professor of theology at the Free University. Let me also express my pleasure at being invited to share this occasion with him by delivering a public lecture on the overall topic that he has chosen, 'Religious Diversity: Philosophical Perspectives.' It will be evident to everybody here that Professor Grube could not have chosen a more timely topic, timely both for you in Europe and for us in North America.

Professor Grube opens the inaugural lecture that he will be giving later today by remarking, 'Tolerance toward other religions than our own is an important commodity.' He then asks, 'But what reasons are there for being tolerant?' He has put his finger on the fundamental question in this area. Religious toleration is important. But why be tolerant? What good reasons are there for being tolerant? The answer to this question that I will propose is different from, but compatible with, the one that Professor Grube will develop in his lecture.

## The nature of toleration

I begin with some brief remarks on the nature of toleration. Suppose that I am Protestant and that you are Catholic. Suppose, further, that though it is not a matter of indifference to me that I am Protestant rather than Catholic – I strongly prefer being Protestant – it is a matter of indifference to me that you are Catholic rather than Protestant. I just do not care.

In that case, I do not tolerate your Catholicism. My indifference means that the issue of whether or not I should tolerate your religion does not even arise. Indifference makes toleration irrelevant. That is not true just for religion; it is true for mundane matters as well. Suppose it is a matter of indifference to me whether you communicate with me by email or by phone. Suppose further that you communicate with me by email. My indifference means that the issue of whether or not I should tolerate your preferred method of communication does not arise.

Change the imagined example. Suppose that, rather than being indifferent to your Catholicism, I prize it. 'So interesting to have a Catholic in the neighborhood. Being surrounded by nothing but Protestants and secularists was getting to be so boring.' If I prize your Catholicism, I do not tolerate it. When John Stuart Mill urged that disagreement be prized on the ground that the clash of opinions makes the attainment of truth more likely, he was not urging toleration of disagreement. (It is a nice question to what extent Mill prized disagreement by others with his views!)

A good deal of what passes for religious toleration in the Western world today is not toleration of religious diversity but indifference. It should be added, however, that very few people are indifferent to all religious diversity. The liberal Christian who not only tolerates but prizes having a progressive Hindu in the neighborhood is likely to be upset if a right-wing American evangelical Christian moves in. Being upset by having the evangelical Christian in the neighborhood offers him/her an opportunity to practice religious toleration; his/her prizing having the progressive Hindu in the neighborhood does not offer him/her an opportunity to practice religious toleration.

What is required for tolerating your religious beliefs and practices is that, rather than prizing them or being indifferent, I must, for some reason, dislike or disapprove them. My dislike or disapproval can range all the way from mild to intense; but your religious beliefs and practices must for some reason concern me negatively if toleration is to enter the picture. Given that there is something about your religious beliefs and practices that I dislike or disapprove of, I can then decide whether or not to 'put up with' them. To put up with them is to tolerate them.

I may put up with them in certain ways and not in others. While being opposed to making it illegal for you to practice your religion, I may shun you on account of your religion, ridicule you, mock you, advocate that you not be treated equally with the rest of us by the state, and so forth. In being opposed to making it illegal for you to practice your religion I am, so far forth, putting up with your religion. In nonetheless shunning you on account of your religion, I am not putting up with it. My behavior is a mixture of toleration and lack of toleration.

Notice that tolerating your religious beliefs and practices in a certain way becomes a live option for me only if I believe that my own religion and morality permit me to tolerate them in that way. Therein lies the greatest obstacle to religious toleration: many religious people, down through the ages and yet today, believe that their religion obligates them not to tolerate other religions. God demands that heresy be stamped out. Allah demands that idols be destroyed and the infidel be eliminated. The emergence of widespread religious toleration in the West required a deep alteration in the religious mentality of Western Christians.

Before I leave my opening topic of the nature of toleration, let me bring into the picture what Professor Grube, in his lecture, calls 'the classical pluralist paradigm' of religious diversity. According to this paradigm, all religions – or at least all axial religions – are alike in a fundamental way, their differences being variations on that commonality. Those who hold this paradigm add that the variations are, for the most part, of equal worth. Different theorists have developed the paradigm in different ways; Grube singles out John Hick and Paul Knitter. Hick's idea was that all axial religions are adumbrations of the 'Real as such' and equally valid responses to their adumbrations; they all provide paths to salvation. Knitter's thought was that at the core of all axial religions is commitment to what he called 'eco-human justice,' by which he means well-being for human beings in general and for the poor in particular, and well-being for our endangered planet Earth.

Grube offers some astute criticisms of these two examples of the classical pluralist paradigm. The question raised by my discussion of the nature of religious toleration is whether those who espouse some version of the paradigm are urging that we be indifferent to religious diversity or that we be tolerant of it. Quite clearly the answer is the former. If I regard your religion as an equally good adumbration of the 'Real as such' as my religion, and equally good as a path to salvation, then I will be indifferent to the fact that you do not share my religion. I may well continue to prefer my own religion; but the fact that yours is different from mine will not bother me. And if it does not in some way bother me, the issue of my tolerating your religion does not arise. Those who espouse some version of the classical pluralist paradigm sometimes advertise it as a way to achieve religious toleration. I think it is not that. It is a way to achieve religious indifference.

## A bit of history

Before I present my own rationale for religious toleration, let me insert a bit of history. For approximately a thousand years, from roughly the middle of the seventh century to roughly the middle of the seventeenth, it was far and away the dominant view in the West that it belonged to the calling of the civil magistrate to promote and protect public forms of Christian piety. John Calvin's statement was typical. He wrote: civil government not only sees to it 'that men breathe, eat, drink, and are kept warm.' It also 'prevents idolatry, sacrilege against God's name, blasphemies against his truth, and other public offenses against religion from arising and spreading among the people' (*Institutes* IV.xx.3).[1] Thus it was that Calvin went along with the decision of the authorities in Geneva to execute Servetus, though not with their decision to do so by burning at the stake. The heresy of Servetus had to be prevented from spreading. As historians have often noted, most other European authorities would have done the same had Servetus wandered into their jurisdiction.

So what accounts for the change from governmental intolerance of religious diversity to the governmental toleration that was encapsulated in the first amendment to the US Constitution: 'Congress shall make no law respecting an establishment of religion, or prohibiting the free exercise thereof'? Two things, I would say.

First, the European wars of religion waged in the sixteenth and early seventeenth century, provoked by the fracturing of religious unity represented by the Reformation, persuaded a good many people that the price being paid in blood by attempts to maintain or reestablish religious unity was too high a price; it was not worth it.

This consequentialist argument for religious toleration was never more eloquently stated than it was in a well-known pamphlet written in French that appeared in 1579, *A Discourse upon the Permission of Freedom of Religion, called Religions-Vrede in the Netherlands*. Though the author presents himself as Catholic, the predominance of scholarly opinion nowadays holds that he was the prominent Huguenot, Philip du Plessis Mornay. Here is what he wrote:

> I ask those who do not want to admit the two religions in this country how they now intend to abolish one of them…. It goes without saying that you cannot abolish any religious practice without using force and taking up arms, and going to war against each other instead of taking up arms in unison against Don John and his adherents and delivering us from the insupportable tyranny of the foreigners. If we intend to ruin the Protestants we will ruin ourselves, as

the French did. The conclusion to be drawn from this is that it would be better to live in peace with them, rather than ruin ourselves by internal discord and carry on a hazardous, disastrous, long and difficult war or rather a perpetual and impossible one. Taking everything into consideration, we can choose between two things: we can either allow them to live in peace with us or we can all die together; we can either let them be or, desiring to destroy them, be ourselves destroyed by their ruin... . As we cannot forbid these people to practise their religion without starting a war and cannot destroy them by that war without being destroyed ourselves let us conclude that we must let them live in peace and grant them liberty... .[2]

At roughly the same time that this consequentialist argument for religious toleration was gaining widespread acceptance, a certain understanding of true religion that led to the same conclusion was also gaining widespread acceptance. In the decade beginning in 1776, all the newly-freed American colonies composed constitutions in which the civil right to free exercise of religion was guaranteed. With the exception of the constitution of the State of New York, this civil right to free exercise of religion was based on the understanding of religion that was newly gaining acceptance. This understanding comes to expression more fully and lucidly in the Pennsylvania Constitution of 1776 than in any other; let me quote:

> That all men have a natural and unalienable right to worship Almighty God according to the dictates of their own consciences and understanding: And that no man ought or of right can be compelled to attend any religious worship, or erect or support any place of worship, or maintain any ministry, contrary to, or against, his own free will and consent... . And that no authority can or ought to be vested in, or assumed by any power whatever that shall in any case interfere with, or in any manner control, the right of conscience in the free exercise of religious worship.

Everyone has a natural right to be free to worship God according to the dictates of his or her own conscience; hence, everyone should have the civil right to do so. That is the argument. Along with the consequentialist argument, it was the spread of this argument, and the spread of the view of religion implicit in the argument, that led to widespread calls for religious toleration.

True religion is the worship of God according to the dictates of one's own conscience. It is a very different view of religion from that which came to expression in the passage I quoted from Calvin. Though it was not until the eighteenth century that it gained prominence in the West, it can be traced all the way back into some of the Church Fathers. Here, for example, is what the Latin Church Father, Lactantius, said on the matter:

> [N]othing is so much a matter of free will as religion. The worship of God... requires full commitment and faith. For how will God love the worshipper if He Himself is not loved by him, or grant to the petitioner whatever he asks when he draws near and offers his prayer without sincerity or reverence. But [the pagans], when they come to offer sacrifice, offer to their gods nothing from within, nothing of themselves, no innocence of mind, no reverence, no awe. (*Divine Institutes* V.20)[3]

Unlike the US state constitutions of the late eighteenth century, Lactantius does not speak of the natural right to be free to worship God according to one's own religious convictions. He speaks, instead, of the sort of worship that God requires: God requires that worship be the free expression of one's inner commitment and reverence. The implicit understanding of true religion is the same, however. True religion is an expression of one's inner convictions and devotion. And since those cannot be forced, true religion cannot be forced.

## Introducing the dignity argument for religious toleration

I turn now to my own argument for religious toleration. As I noted earlier, religious toleration takes many different forms. It takes the form of the government granting you free exercise of your religion. It takes the form of my interacting with you socially in spite of my disapproval of your religion. It takes the form of my doing business with you in spite of my disapproval of your religion. And so forth. Rather than trying to keep in mind the many different forms that religious toleration can take, let me simplify things by focusing on the first form that I just now mentioned, namely, toleration by the government in the form of allowing free exercise of all religions. At the completion of the argument I will make a brief remark about its application to other forms of toleration.

The argument that I will present for governmental toleration resembles the argument found in those US state constitutions that I mentioned, in that it too is a rights-argument. Indeed, I think that the argument I will present can be seen as a fleshing-out of the rights-argument that one finds there.

On this occasion, let me assume, without argument, that there are rights and that they are grounded in the worth or dignity of the rights-holder. Let me also assume, without argument, that there are natural rights – that is, rights not conferred on rights-holders by laws, social practices, or speech actions. I know, of course, that both of these assumptions are highly controversial. I have defended them at length elsewhere.[4]

If there are some among you who are dubious about them, I invite you to adopt a hypothetical attitude toward the argument that follows. Suppose that there are natural rights, and suppose that they are grounded in the worth or dignity of the rights-holder: What reason might there be for holding that among our natural rights there is a natural right to toleration of one's religion in the form of government allowing one to exercise one's religion freely?

## An understanding of religion

For my purposes here, I need an account of religion. If I offered my own account, I might be charged with stacking the decks in favor of my argument. So let me instead employ the account that Thomas Nagel offers of what he calls the 'religious temperament' in his book, *Secular Philosophy and the Religious Temperament*.

The religious temperament, says Nagel, is the belief 'that there is some kind of all-encompassing mind or spiritual principle in addition to the minds of individual human beings and other creatures – and that this mind or spirit is the foundation of the existence of the universe, of the natural order, of value, and of our existence, nature, and purpose.'[5] The religious temperament is the 'belief in such a conception of the universe, and the incorporation of that belief into one's conception of oneself and one's life.' The religious temperament addresses 'the question of how a human individual can live in harmony with the universe.'[6]

In Nagel's explanation of the religious temperament, belief is prominent. We can debate whether belief does have the prominence in the religious temperament that Nagel gives it. More important for my purposes here, however, is that a person's religion should not be identified with his/her religious temperament, however one understands that. His/her religion is his/her religious temperament along with his/her way of giving expression to that temperament in his/her way of living, including his/her religious practices. A person's religion is his/her particular way of living 'in harmony with the universe.' The beliefs comprised within his/her religious temperament will often be implicit within his/her way of living rather than consciously entertained.

I judge that everything covered by this account would naturally be called a religion; whether it is also the case that everything that would naturally be called a religion is covered by this account is perhaps less clear. But whatever one concludes on that matter will not make a difference to my argument. Opponents of religion often speak as if it were some quirky add-on to what science and common sense tell us, a relic of the childhood of the human race. On Nagel's description, it is anything but that. Our question now is whether, and in what way, depriving a person of the freedom to practice his/her religion constitutes treating him/her in a way that does not befit him/her worth, and hence violates his/her rights.

## Why the standard way of trying to ground natural rights is inadequate

Most present-day thinkers who hold both that there are natural rights and that these are grounded in the worth or dignity of the rights-holder are of the view that what imparts to the rights-holder the relevant dignity is the capacity for rational agency – that is, the capacity to act for reasons and not just from causes. Some hold the more specific view that the dignity in question is grounded in the capacity for *normative* agency – that is, in the capacity to perform an action for the reason that one judges it to be a good or obligatory thing for one to do. This is the view defended, for example, by James Griffin in his book *On Human Rights*. He urges his readers to 'see human rights as protections of our normative agency.'[7]

I have argued in a number of places that this account of the dignity that grounds natural rights is inadequate.[8] Obviously it does not account for the dignity of those human beings who are not capable of functioning as persons and who, accordingly, lack the capacity for normative agency – infants, for example, and those in a permanent coma or suffering from the final stages of Alzheimer's disease.

More relevant to our purposes here, the rational agency explanation of dignity also fails to account for a good many of the rights possessed by those who are fully capable of functioning as persons. For example, it does not account for the right not to have one's privacy invaded. Suppose that someone invades your privacy but does nothing with what he learns other than enjoy it at home, thus in no way impairing your agency. You have nonetheless been wronged; your rights have been violated. You have a right not to have your privacy invaded.

Neither does the rational agency explanation of dignity account for the right not to be raped or castrated. Rape and castration do indeed constitute an impairment of one's normative agency; but I find it grotesque to suggest that this is what is fundamentally wrong with such misdeeds. They are gross violations of a person's bodily integrity.

We can agree that rational and normative agency give to those human beings who possess such agency great worth and dignity. But what is indicated by the examples I have offered, along with a good many others, is that what gives to human beings the worth and dignity on which supervene the natural rights that we have qua persons has to be more than just the capacity for rational and normative agency. To account for natural rights we need a richer understanding of what it is to be a human person.

## A richer understanding of persons

Here is not the place to present an understanding of the human person rich enough to account for the dignity that grounds the full panoply of the natural rights that we have qua persons.[9] Let me confine myself to singling out two aspects of the human person, in addition to the capacities for rational and normative agency, that are directly relevant to the natural right to free exercise of one's religion.[10]

1. To be a human person is to have the capacity to interpret reality and one's place therein. Some of these interpretations happen naturally, as in perception and introspection; I just naturally interpret what is presented to me as the sun rising above the horizon. In our capacity for such interpretations, we are similar to some of the animals. But to be a human person is also to have the capacity for interpretations that are not given with our nature and go far beyond perceptual and introspective interpretation. We interpret what is happening as the gods being angry, as the far-flung effects of the Big Bang, as the dire effects of the spread of libertarianism among the populace, and so forth. Interpretations such as these go vastly beyond perceptual and introspective interpretation and are optional, in the sense that some human beings interpret reality in these ways and some do not.

As for myself, I cannot imagine what it would be like not to have the capacity for such interpretations of reality and of my place therein; it is a pervasive and fundamental part of my life, so pervasive and fundamental that I hardly ever take note of it. I take it for granted. But when I do stand back and take note of it, I find it remarkable, amazing. If any of the non-human animals have this hermeneutic capacity, or something like it, they have it only to a minimal degree.

2. To be a full-fledged human person is also to have the capacity to form what I shall call a 'valorized identity.' What I mean by the 'valorized identity' of a person is the relative importance that he/she assigns to states and events in his/her life: to his/her various beliefs, to his/her various commitments, to his/her plans for action, his/her memories, his/her attachments to persons, animals, and objects, and so forth. We say such things as, 'This commitment is more important to me than any other; I cannot imagine giving it up. It is fundamental to who I am.' Thereby one is verbalizing one aspect of one's valorized identity. One's valorized identity consists not of the importance one assigns to things outside oneself but, to repeat, to the various states and events in one's own life.

As for myself, I cannot imagine what it would be like not to have the capacity to form my own valorized identity; it, too, is a pervasive and fundamental part of my life, so much so that I hardly ever take note of it. I take it for granted. But when I do stand back and take note of it, I find it remarkable, amazing. If any of the non-human animals have this valorizing capacity, or something like it, they have it only to a minimal degree.

I have stressed that these two capacities are amazing. On account of possessing these hermeneutic and valorizing capacities, along with those of rational and normative agency and others that I have not mentioned, human persons are remarkable, amazing. So far as we know, no other creatures that dwell on earth possess these capacities to anywhere near the same degree, if, indeed, they possess them at all. Not only are human persons remarkable on account of possessing these capacities, they also have great worth on account of possessing them. On account of possessing these hermeneutic and valorizing capacities, along with others, human persons are precious. They have multifaceted dignity. They are to be prized. Something of great worth is lost when these capacities are destroyed or lost.

**The dignity argument for religious toleration**

Religions represent a remarkable exercise of these two capacities, along, of course, with the capacities for rational and normative agency. To see this, let me again quote Nagel's description of the religious temperament. The religious temperament is the belief 'that there is some kind of all-encompassing mind or spiritual principle in addition to the minds of individual human beings and other creatures – and that this mind or spirit is the foundation of the existence of the universe, of the natural order, of value, and of our existence, nature, and purpose.' The religious temperament is the 'belief in such a conception of the universe and the incorporation of that belief into one's conception of oneself and one's life.' The religious temperament addresses 'the question of how a human individual can live in harmony with the universe.' I suggested that we think of a person's religion as his/her religious temperament along with his/her way of giving expression to that temperament in his/her life and practices, especially his/her religious practices.

It is obvious that religion, so understood, is a manifestation of the hermeneutic and valorizing capacities that I identified, along with those of rational and moral agency. A person's religion includes the belief that there is some kind of all-encompassing mind or spirit that is the foundation of the existence of the universe, of value, and of our own existence, nature, and purpose. Such a belief is obviously a manifestation of the remarkable and precious capacity for interpretation that I took note of above. A person's religion is not just that belief, however, but includes his/her way of giving expression to that belief in life and practice. That will perforce be an exercise of the person's capacity for forming a valorized identity.

Given that those who possess these two remarkable capacities, along with the capacity for rational and normative agency, have great worth on that account, they have a natural right to be treated in ways that befit that worth. And being treated in ways that befit that worth will quite obviously include having the civil right to free exercise of their religions.

Let me immediately add that that civil right is a *prima facie* right, not an all-things-considered right. No one whose religion includes child sacrifice should have the civil right to practice his religion freely.


**Other applications of the dignity argument for religious toleration**

It would be worth exploring applications of the dignity argument for religious toleration in addition to the application on which I have focused attention, namely, governmental toleration in the form of the civil right to free exercise. For example, is paying due respect to the dignity of a person compatible with refusing to employ him/her in one's business because one does not like his/her religion? Is it compatible with avoiding social contact with him/her because one does not like his/her religion? Does it require, on the contrary, that one be willing to engage in religious dialogue with that person? Arriving at well-considered answers to these and similar questions would take a good deal of time and effort; it will, accordingly, have to await some other occasion.

I would, however, like to make a brief comment about inter-religious dialogue. It is rather often said or assumed that the aim of dialogue between or among those of different religions should be to find common ground. That seems to me a mistake. It is not a mistake to explore common ground; what is a mistake, as I see it, is to set finding common ground as the sole goal of religious dialogue. When we engage in inter-religious dialogue, we should also state and explore our differences. I do not treat some Jewish acquaintance with due dignity if I say to him: 'I do not want to hear about what makes Judaism distinct from Christianity and why you think those distinctives are important; I only want to hear about what Judaism shares in common with Christianity.'

## In conclusion

In conclusion, let me say just a word about the relation between the argument for religious toleration that I have presented and the argument that Professor Grube will be presenting in his lecture. The argument that I have presented is a rights- and dignity-based argument. The argument that Professor Grube will be presenting is an epistemological argument.

Grube's case for religious toleration is based on two fundamental epistemological claims.

First, religious beliefs are of such a sort that they are never certain for one. One may *feel* certain; lots of religious believers do feel certain of their beliefs. But that is different from those beliefs *being* certain for them. One can be certain that $5 + 3 = 8$; so too one can be certain that one is in pain when one is. Religious beliefs, in general, are not like those; they are neither self-evident necessary truths nor are they reports of states of consciousness. They are indeterminate, in the sense that one is not in a position to determine their truth with anything like certainty.

Second, I may be fully entitled in holding some religious belief *P* and you may be fully entitled in believing the contradictory of *P*. That is to say, I may be blameless in believing *P*, in the sense that there is no practice of inquiry that I ought to have employed but did not employ such that, had I employed it, I would not believe *P;* but you may likewise be blameless in believing *not-P*. That is because entitlement is very much context-dependent, as truth is not.

Suppose, now, that I discover that you believe the contradictory of some religious belief, *P*, that I hold. Presumably I also believe, or take for granted, that I am entitled to my belief *P*. And now suppose that I conclude, after some investigation, that you are likewise entitled to your belief *not-P*. Does it follow that I should tolerate your belief that I should put up with it? It does not. My conclusion, that you are blameless in believing *not-P*, is certainly a good *prima facie* reason for my tolerating your belief. But it is no more than a *prima facie* reason; it is not an all-things-considered reason. I may judge that your belief, entitled though you are to hold it, is truly appalling, profoundly racist, or whatever. In that circumstance, it may well be that I should not tolerate it. Recall that dignity reasons for religious toleration are also *prima facie* reasons.

So here is where things stand: by the time this conference concludes, you will have been presented with two kinds of arguments for religious toleration. The arguments are very different: one is moral, the other is epistemological. But they are compatible. It may well be that I should tolerate the religion of someone other than myself both for the moral reason that I have suggested and for the epistemological reason that Professor Grube will suggest.

## Notes

1. Battles translation, 1488.
2. du Plessis Mornay, "Discourse sur la Permission de Liberté de Religion," 163.
3. Unpublished translation by Robert Wilken.
4. See Wolterstorff, *Justice: Rights and Wrongs*.
5. Nagel, *Secular Philosophy and the Religious Temperament*, 5.
6. Ibid.

7. Griffin, *On Human Rights*, 33.
8. See, in particular, *Justice: Rights and Wrongs*.
9. I have attempted that in Chapter 8 of Wolterstorff, *Understanding Liberal Democracy*.
10. The thought comes to mind that perhaps these two capacities should be incorporated into a more comprehensive understanding of rational and normative agency. I think not. Neither one is, strictly speaking, a capacity for agency.

## Bibliography

Calvin, J. *Institutes of the Christian Religion*. Translated by Ford Lewis Battles. Philadelphia: Westminster Press, 1967.

du Plessis Mornay, P. "Discourse sur la Permission de Liberté de Religion, Dicte Religions-Vrede au Pays Bas (1559)." In *Texts Concerning the Revolt of the Netherlands*, Translated and edited by E. H. Kossman and A. F. Mellink. Cambridge: Cambridge University Press, 1974.

Griffin, J. *On Human Rights*. Oxford: Oxford University Press, 2008.

Nagel, T. *Secular Philosophy and the Religious Temperament*. Oxford: Oxford University Press, 2010.

Wolterstorff, N. *Justice: Rights and Wrongs*. Princeton: Princeton University Press, 2008.

Wolterstorff, N. *Understanding Liberal Democracy*. Oxford: Oxford University Press, 2012.

# Conflations and gaps. A response to Nicholas Wolterstorff's 'toleration, justice, and dignity'

Christoph Baumgartner

This contribution responds to Nicholas Wolterstorff's argument for religious toleration and freedom of religion respectively that he develops in his paper 'Toleration, justice and dignity'. I argue that Wolterstorff conflates religious toleration and the right to freedom of religion, which has problematic implications. Moreover, I reveal gaps in his justification of the special worth or dignity of human persons, and, derived from this, freedom of religion.

Nicholas Wolterstorff's paper 'Toleration, justice and dignity' attempts to provide an argument for a specific form of religious toleration, namely the 'natural right to toleration of one's religion in the form of government allowing one to exercise one's religion freely'.[1] In my response to Wolterstorff's paper I want to address two parts of his argument. My first comment concerns his use of the concepts religious toleration on the one hand and freedom of religion on the other. Here, I argue that Wolterstorff conflates religious toleration and the right to freedom of religion, which has problematic implications. My second comment consists of a set of two (critical) remarks concerning Wolterstorff's justification of the special worth or dignity of human persons, and, derived from this, freedom of religion.

## 1. Religious toleration and/or freedom of religion

Wolterstorff conceptualizes religious toleration as putting up with somebody's religious beliefs and practices that the person who tolerates dislikes or disapproves of. In other words, it is essential for toleration that the belief or practice that is tolerated is in one way or the other considered objectionable, wrong or bad. This 'objection component'[2] is part and parcel of toleration; without it we could speak of indifference or appreciation, both of which differ from toleration in important respects. This part of Wolterstorff's definition is in line with dominant liberal conceptualizations of toleration.[3] It is noteworthy, however, that Wolterstorff doesn't conceptually distinguish religious toleration from the right to freedom of religion, but understands the latter as a specific form of religious toleration, on which he focuses in his paper, namely religious toleration in 'the form of the government granting you free exercise of your religion.'[4] In so doing, Wolterstorff construes the state and the government respectively as putting up with, but also as disapproving of religion, be it religion in general or particular religious beliefs and practices. In other words, the state is understood in Wolterstorff's argumentation as explicitly taking a negative judgmental stance to (particular) religions. This is at least in tension with interpretations of freedom of religion, according to which the right to religious liberty is – unlike toleration – inextricably linked with equality and non-discrimination, which requires the state to operate in a non-discriminatory manner in matters of religion.[5] This is very clear in the formulation of the First Amendment to the constitution of the U.S.A. to which Wolterstorff refers (in my view incorrectly) as an example of governmental *toleration*: 'Congress shall make no law respecting an establishment of religion, or prohibiting the free exercise thereof.'[6]

One could object against my criticism of Wolterstorff's conflation of religious toleration and freedom of religion that freedom of religion and religious toleration can easily go together on the level of state politics if one construes the principles of equality and non-discrimination as merely requiring the state not to formally implement its disapproval of religion and particular religions respectively by means of legal regulation. A state could legally allow all citizens to exercise their religion, and at the same time state institutions, including the government, could take up a negative stance on one or several particular religions or forms of religious subjectivity, and act upon it in settings and practices that are not legally regulated as far as religion is concerned. A government could, for example, informally express its appreciation of 'liberal' forms of religion by inviting their religious leaders to important commissions etc. but not those of more traditional or countercultural religious groups.[7] In fact, this may describe the real international politics of religious freedom much better than the idea of an ostensibly 'religiously neutral' state.[8] However, recent debates about a 'Judeo-Christian culture' in Europe, the Swiss ban on minarets, or the (in)famous Lautsi case illustrate very clearly that such cases cannot be adequately treated with reference to religious toleration.[9] The issue of such controversies is not merely the question whether or not religious people should be allowed to practice their religion even if this requires legal exemptions from otherwise valid rules (ritual slaughter is a well-known example thereof); rather, such controversies concern the character of the shared public space and the society itself. Some strategies of religious accommodation (like allowing ritual slaughter) are consistent with religious toleration including its objection component, and they may suffice to ensure one of the essential aims of freedom of religion, namely to allow people to choose and practice their religion freely without coercion by the state, church, or other institutions. However, as soon as the state applies religious toleration to the second type of cases, it is bound to take side with one (form of) religion, and not others, since the claims of different religious or non-religious groups about shaping the public space that all parties have to share often rival with each other. Accordingly, a second important aim of freedom of religion cannot be achieved, namely 'the creation of a polity in which one's economic, civil, legal, or political status is unaffected by one's religious beliefs.'[10] It may be ambitious for a state to prevent the creation of 'second class citizens' whose religion is construed as 'foreign' or 'minority' and to aspire towards the inclusion of members of various religions as fully recognized citizens. It is, however, an implication of a robust conception of freedom of religion to direct politics in this way. Religious toleration doesn't do this, and this is why Wolterstorff's conflation of religious toleration and freedom of religion hampers thorough political philosophical analyses of religious diversity rather than that it would provide a justification of a fundamental normative principle of liberal and religiously diverse societies.

In the remainder of this paper, I will use the term freedom of religion without distinguishing it from religious toleration, because the distinction doesn't affect my criticism of Wolterstorff's justification strategy.

## 2. Wolterstorff's justification of dignity and freedom of religion

Wolterstorff attempts to justify freedom of religion as a natural right that is grounded in the worth or dignity of the rights-holder.[11] His justification strategy can be reconstructed very roughly in two parts. First, Wolterstorff identifies two aspects of the human person that he considers directly relevant to 'the natural right to the free exercise of religion',[12] namely the capacity to interpret reality and one's place therein, and the capacity to form a valorized identity. Human persons, Wolterstorff asserts, have great worth on account of possessing these capacities. The second part of the argument says that religions represent a remarkable exercise of these two capacities, and because of this persons who possess these capacities not only have great worth on that account, but they also have a natural right to be treated in ways that befit that worth – and according to Wolterstorff, this will 'quite obviously' include having the civil right to free exercise of their religion.[13]

Although this reconstruction of Wolterstorff's argument is admittedly rough, it provides sufficient possibilities for comments and critical questions. Let me address two parts that I consider especially noteworthy (1), and in need of further clarification (2), respectively.

### 2.1. Freedom of religion as a right of persons, not a human right

Wolterstorff bases the special worth and dignity, in which the right to freedom of religion is grounded, on specific capacities that he ascribes to human persons, not to human beings in general. The argument cannot show that people who don't possess these capacities (e.g. small children, or people in permanent coma) do also have such special worth. Accordingly, Wolterstorff conceptualizes freedom of religion not as a human right, but as a natural right of persons; all human persons, and only human persons have the capacity to interpret reality and their place therein, and the capacity to form a valorized identity. These capacities, Wolterstorff argues, make human persons and only human persons especially worthy, and freedom of religion is grounded in this worth. If the argument is sound (see below), it justifies the right to freedom of religion only for human persons, not for other humans such as small children. This isn't problematic as long as one understands religion as a practice that depends on capacities such as those outlined by Nicholas Wolterstorff, since every human being will have the right to freedom of religion as soon as he or she is able to make use of it. And actually, such an account is consistent with the UN Convention on the Rights of the Child that states in Article 14 that state parties shall respect the right of the child to freedom of thought, conscience and religion, but qualifies this right by requiring state parties to 'respect the rights and duties of the parents and, when applicable, legal guardians, to provide direction to the child in the exercise of his or her right in a manner consistent with the evolving capacities of the child.' It is noteworthy, however, since the dependency of freedom of religion on specific capacities of persons poses challenges to the inclusion of religions that do not easily accord with an understanding of religion in the sense of Thomas Nagel's 'religious temperament', which almost exclusively emphasizes beliefs and cognitive aspects of religion, and disregards other dimensions of religion, such as embodied beliefs, almost entirely.

## 2.2. *Why do human persons have great worth on account of specific capacities?*

A closer look at Wolterstorff's argument reveals that this question cannot be answered easily. Having described the capacity to interpret reality and one's place therein, and the capacity to form a valorized identity Wolterstorff asserts that if he (!) takes note of these capacities, and reflects upon them, he finds them 'remarkable, amazing'. Please notice that he uses the first person singular, here: 'I [Nicholas Wolterstorff] find it [the capacity] remarkable, amazing.'[14] Later, however, he continues as follows: 'I have stressed that these two capacities *are* amazing.' Here, Wolterstorff does not use the first person singular, but simply asserts the amazingness of the capacities *as a matter of fact*. And even more, he asserts that human persons are remarkable and amazing on account of possessing these capacities, and that means, according to Wolterstorff, that human persons have great worth, are precious, and have dignity. So, to put it a bit polemically, the argument seems to say that somebody or something has great worth because of the fact that somebody (Nicholas Wolterstorff) finds it amazing – all the rest follows as it were by implication. I do understand that Wolterstorff doesn't want to argue that the simple fact that he or some other person finds something remarkable and amazing bestows special worth on somebody or something.[15] But there is a missing link that justifies the leap from a personal experience of somebody ('somebody experiences something X as amazing') to a normative statement that claims to be valid for other people, as well ('X has special worth or dignity and deserves to be protected'). Without further clarification, this missing link knocks down Wolterstorff's strategy to justify the right to freedom of religion with reference to the capacities to interpret reality and one's place therein, and to form a valorized identity.

### Notes

1. Wolterstorff, "Toleration, Justice and Dignity," 381.
2. Forst, *Toleration in Conflict*, 18.
3. See, e.g., Forst, *Toleration in Conflict* and Galeotti, *Toleration as Recognition*.
4. Wolterstorff, "Toleration, Justice and Dignity," 381.
5. See Bielefeldt, "Freedom of Religion or Belief," and Ceva, "Why Toleration is not the Appropriate Response."
6. Wolterstorff, "Toleration, Justice and Dignity," 379.
7. I borrow the concept of countercultural religious groups from S.E. Mumford who characterizes such groups as groups that define themselves in terms of separateness and distinctiveness. See Mumford, "The Judicial Resolution".
8. See Winnifred Faller Sulivan's influential book *The Impossibility of Religious Freedom*, contributions in Sullivan e.a. *Politics of Religious Freedom*, and the recent works of Hurd, *Beyond Religious Freedom* and Mahmood, *Religious Difference in a Secular Age*.
9. On the Lautsi case see Tempermann, *The Lautsi Papers*, an analysis of the Swiss ban on minarets in the light of a 'liberal nationalism' is provided by Miller, "Majorities and Minarets". For the construction of the concept of a Judeo-Christian culture see Hemel, "(Pro)Claiming Tradition".
10. Mahmood, "Religious Freedom," 418.
11. Wolterstorff, "Toleration, Justice and Dignity," 381.
12. Ibid., 389.
13. Ibid., 384.
14. Ibid., 383.
15. On bestowed worth see Wolterstorff, *Justice*, 357.

## Bibliography

Bielefeldt, H. "Freedom of Religion or Belief – A Human Right under Pressure." *Oxford Journal of Law and Religion* 1 (2012): 15–35. doi:10.1093/ojlr/rwr018.

Ceva, E. "Why Toleration Is Not the Appropriate Response to Dissenting Minorities' Claims." *European Journal of Philosophy* 23, no. 3 (2012): 633–651. doi:10.1111/j.1468-0378.2012.00563.x.

Forst, R. *Toleration in Conflict. Past and Present.* Cambridge: Cambridge University Press, 2013.

Galeotti, A. E. *Toleration as Recognition.* Cambridge: Cambridge University Press, 2005.

Hemel, E. V. D. "(Pro)Claiming Tradition: The 'Judeo-Christian' Roots of Dutch Society and the Rise of Conservative Nationalism." In *Postsecular Publics*, edited by R. Braidotti, B. Blaegaard, T. de Graauw, and E. Midden, 53–76. Basingstoke: Palgrave MacMillan, 2014.

Hurd, E. S. *Beyond Religious Freedom. The New Global Politics of Religion.* Princeton: Princeton University Press, 2015.

Mahmood, S. "Religious Freedom, the Minority Question, and Geopolitics in the Middle East." *Comparative Studies in Society and History* 54, no. 2 (2012): 418–446. doi:10.1017/S0010417512000096.

Mahmood, S. *Religious Difference in a Secular Age. A Minority Report.* Princeton: Princeton University Press, 2015.

Miller, D. "Majorities and Minarets: Religious Freedom and Public Space." *British Journal of Political Science* (2015). doi:10.1017/S0007123414000131.

Mumford, S. E. "The Judicial Resolution of Disputes Involving Children and Religion." *International and Comparative Law Quarterly* 47, no. 01 (1998): 117–148. doi:10.1017/S0020589300061583.

Sullivan, W. F. *The Impossibility of Religious Freedom.* Princeton: Princeton University Press, 2005.

Sullivan, W. F. e.a. eds. *Politics of Religious Freedom.* Chicago: The University of Chicago Press, 2015.

Tempermann, J., ed. *The Lautsi Papers: Multidisciplinary Reflections on Religious Symbols in the Public School Classroom.* Leiden: Brill/Martinus Nijhoff, 2012.

Tiedemann, P. "Is There a Human Right to Freedom of Religion?" *Human Rights Review* 16 (2015): 83–98. doi:10.1007/s12142-014-0342-2.

Wolterstorff, N. "Toleration, Justice and Dignity. Lecture on the occasion of the inauguration as professor of Dirk-Martin Grube at Free University of Amsterdam, 2015, September 24." *International Journal of Philosophy and Theology* 76, no. 5 (2015): 377–386.

Wolterstorff, N. *Justice. Rights and Wrongs.* Princeton: Princeton University Press, 2008.

# Tolerant because Christianity itself is a hybrid tradition: a response to Nicholas Wolterstorff's 'Toleration, Justice and Dignity'

Maarten Wisse

In Nicholas Wolterstorff's 'Toleration, Justice and Dignity', he argues for tolerance between religious traditions on the basis of human dignity. In this response to his paper, I argue that a general philosophical argument from human dignity will at best lead to indifference or mere praise, but not true tolerance. In the second part of the paper, I offer a sketch of a distinctly Christian way of arguing for tolerance towards adherents of other religions, namely on the basis of the insight that Christianity itself is a hybrid tradition.

In the beginning of his paper, Nicholas Wolterstorff draws attention to a distinction that is important but often overlooked: the difference between tolerance, on the one hand, and indifference and praise on the other hand. As Wolterstorff says: 'What is required for tolerating your religious beliefs and practices is that, rather than praising them or being indifferent, I must, for some reason, dislike or disapprove of them' (378). Be it mild or intense, tolerance implies disagreement or even dislike. I wholly agree.

For theologians who seek to broaden the scope of their expertise to religious traditions other than Christianity and seek to form a dialogical community with these traditions, this has important ramifications. In line with Wolterstorff's concept of religious tolerance as implying disagreement or dislike, we might distinguish between *de facto* diversity and *de jure* diversity. In our society, we live in a situation of *de facto* religious diversity. We live among Muslims, Buddhists, Hindus, and many Christian denominations. But if we intend to form a dialogical community, we have to bring about the transition from *de facto* diversity to *de jure* diversity. If we are going to make religious diversity a part of our cultural DNA, this requires going beyond indifference or praise of diversity and must include disagreement and even dislike. If one never feels irritated, one is not engaging in such a dialogical community. In that case, one either ignores the radical differences in one's environment and celebrates the moderate differences with which one is satisfied, or one has already excluded those who are more radically different than one would allow. Therefore, I also agree with Wolterstorff's (and Grube's) rejection of a pluralist approach to religious diversity because such an approach praises religious diversity irrespective of what that diversity is. In this view, what people believe does not really matter. What matters is that all have a share in the truth.

The question is, then, and this is basically the subject of the rest of Wolterstorff's paper, why we should be tolerant towards members of other religions or even stimulate religious diversity and make it part of our theological DNA. Wolterstorff argues that this is because of human dignity. What makes humans human is their right to think for themselves, to make up their own mind and not be punished for that.

What must be addressed is whether this suffices as a basis for religious tolerance. As Wolterstorff has argued at the beginning of his paper, true tolerance is not the same as indifference or appraisal. It must include disagreement or dislike. The argument from human dignity, however, is of a moral kind and thus makes being tolerant a condition of being morally responsible. I wonder whether such a moral obligation satisfies Wolterstorff's own criterion for true tolerance. When members of one religion disagree with people who hold different religious convictions, does the argument from human dignity suffice to motivate them to be actively tolerant towards them in spite of those differences? Or does it, at best, bring them to indifference or distant appraisal? Would not the most natural response to the obligation of religious tolerance on the basis of human dignity be: 'O really, you're right, these guys have every right to speak up for themselves and be a member of society, but I'm not at all interested in what they believe. As long as they don't enforce their opinions on the whole of society and as long as they don't kill people with other convictions, I don't care.' So, why should the argument from human dignity lead to anything more than religious indifference?

Therefore, my thesis is as follows: for adherents of one religion to become intrinsically motivated to tolerate adherents of other religions, they have to find the grounds for doing so in the core of their own religious conviction. So, rather than developing a general philosophical motivation for religious diversity and religious tolerance, as Wolterstorff has done and as Dirk-Martin Grube does in his inaugural lecture published in this same issue, I would like to urge religious traditions to develop such a motivation from within their traditions. Thus, the motivation for religious tolerance should not be developed philosophically but theologically. Motivations for religious tolerance are intrinsically contextual and relative to one's religious tradition or denomination. They are particular and contextual rather than general.

My argument so far is broadly in line with developments in the theology of religions in the last few decades. After a rather strong critique of pluralism,[1] the theology of religions now emphasizes that religious dialogue and the theology of religions need a grounding in religious traditions themselves.[2] Therefore, different religious traditions cannot develop this grounding in one and the same way. This may even be true of different denominations within a religious tradition.

In the remainder of my response, I shall give a few hints as to what a theological motivation for religious tolerance and an engagement in religious dialogue might look like when developed from a distinctly Christian perspective, more precisely a variety of the Reformed tradition. My argument is a retrieval[3] of the distinction between Law and Gospel that has played a role in the Protestant Reformation and beyond but is no longer so strongly present in contemporary Reformed theology. Quite to the contrary, it is now more often associated with the Lutheran tradition. Historically, however, the use of the distinction was a common feature of the premodern Reformed and Lutheran traditions.[4]

I am well aware of various alternative ways to develop a motivation for tolerance and dialogue from the core of the Christian religion. After the aforementioned critique of pluralist theologies of religions, a whole range of proposals has been put forward for motivating dialogue from a distinctly Christian perspective. Particular attention has been paid to a Trinitarian perspective, and such a perspective has been elaborated in different ways.[5] There is no room here to argue for or against these perspectives. What most approaches have in common is that they draw most of their inspiration from modern theology. My choice to offer a retrieval of a premodern distinction to deal with tolerance towards other religions is partly motivated by an attempt to show that a theology of the religions in favour of tolerance and dialogue can also be construed in terms of premodern theological insights.

As Wolterstorff has rightly noted in his paper, this does not mean that the argument provided below is necessarily in contradiction with others. Nor is a distinctly Christian motivation for tolerance and dialogue necessarily in contradiction with those from other religions. One of the main problems of the traditional distinction between three types of theologies of religions, exclusivism, inclusivism and pluralism, is that it presupposes that religious traditions are internally consistent but mutually exclusive sets of beliefs. This is not necessarily the case. Neither are religious traditions necessarily internally consistent, nor do they necessarily exclude each other.

This leads to the first argument in favour of religious tolerance, dialogue and *de jure* diversity from the Christian tradition: Christianity itself is a product of an intrareligious and, eventually, interreligious dialogue. The Christian tradition is a product of a complex interplay between appeals to the New Testament, which was mostly the central point of reference, and appeals to the Old Testament. On the one hand, we find ways in which the New Testament overrules or complements the Old Testament. On the other hand, we find cases in which the Christian tradition has drawn on the Old Testament, more or less against claims made in the New Testament. The Old Testament has never been rejected from the canon. Quite to the contrary, such rejection has always been condemned as a heresy.[6] Thus, the Holy Scriptures of the Christian religion themselves embody an internal dialectics between two traditions rather than a consistent set of beliefs that excludes all other sets.

This internal dialectics provides an intrinsic motivation for religious tolerance, respect and dialogue. The complex interplay between appeals to both the Old and the New Testaments provide some sort of initial glimpse of the distinction that we are after, although it does not coincide with it. Prima facie, one might take the distinction between Law and Gospel as one between the Old and the New Testaments, but the premodern protestant tradition saw aspects of both Law and Gospel in both parts of the Bible. For them, the fundamental distinction is not between parts of the Bible but a systematic distinction between two ways in which God relates to human beings. According to this distinction, 'Law' refers to everything that God commands, and 'Gospel' refers to everything that God freely offers us by grace alone. As Gisbertus Voetius explains in one of his disputations on Law and Gospel:

> The Gospel, strictly speaking, and insofar as it is distinguished from the law, in itself and directly does not prescribe anything to us, or requires anything from us that we have to do, speaking: do this, or, believe, or, have faith; [...] But it refers to, announces, and signifies to us what Christ has done for us, and what God in Christ promises, what he wants to do, and what he will do.[7]

Premodern Lutheran and Reformed traditions claimed that all that pertains to the Law is given to us in creation and by nature, so that God's giving the Law to Israel and the Church is more like a reminder of something that we already know rather than imposing anything new. In this, they followed the medieval natural law tradition. This should not be interpreted as if all human beings would agree on a specific set of moral prescriptions but in the sense that God's revealed rules for moral behaviour resonate with a natural longing for the good and make an appeal to moral ideals that correspond to the way in which we have been created. One might think of the command to love one another or the insight that human beings have an intrinsic value and, therefore, should not be killed.

It is from the interplay between the Old Testament's and New Testament's callings towards the good and their witness to what God did, does and will do in Christ that I would like to develop an intrinsically Christian motivation for religious tolerance. From this perspective, Christianity itself is a dynamic interplay between insights that resonate with universally human concerns and wisdom, on the one hand, and special revelation of God's work in Christ on the other hand. From this perspective, Christians are not primarily people who believe everything that is said in the Bible, taken together into a consistent and exclusive set of beliefs, but Christians are people who believe in Jesus Christ. This belief in Christ is not without its connection to things to be done; quite to the contrary, it shares a concern about the good life with other religions or secular views of life, and it brings these concerns into an interaction with the centre of its faith in Jesus Christ. A Buddhist view of the good life, for example, might be brought into dialogue with a Christian view of the good life as we find it in the New Testament, but also, as Buddhists and Christians have done, the life of Jesus might be viewed in several ways as reflecting a Buddhist ideal of the good life. At the same time, Christ is not only an ideal of a good life but also the life giving God who enables us to live a good life, and this good news remains different from a Buddhist view of life, however much we may appreciate it from a Christian point of view.

The dynamics internal to the Christian faith is why Christians can be intrinsically motivated to tolerate other religious traditions, respect those traditions and be in an ongoing dialogue with them about the good life. This is because, in their fundamental concern about the good life, Christians are on common ground with these traditions. This does not mean that the purpose of interreligious dialogue is to find out what one has in common, as Wolterstorff rightly criticized. Common ground means an invitation to discover what God has given in other religions through creation and revelation, somewhat similar to the way in which Christianity obliges one to listen to everything written in the Old Testament.

From this perspective, Christianity forbids one to enforce one's faith in Jesus Christ on anyone anywhere, because that would destroy the most fundamental nature of that faith in Jesus Christ as a response to an essentially free offer of grace and salvation in Jesus Christ and would, instead, turn it into an obligation. Christians are invited to tell others about Christ and about what Christians find in him, but they have to proclaim the Gospel as good news, as a free offer, and, thus, they are obliged to tolerate and respect anyone who does not yet accept that offer or who never will.


## Acknowledgement

I would like to thank Marcel Sarot for his comments on an earlier version of this paper.


## Notes

1. D'Costa, *Christian Uniqueness Reconsidered*.
2. Moyaert, *Fragile Identities*.
3. Cf. Webster, "Theologies of Retrieval"; Crisp, *Retrieving Doctrine*, preface.
4. Schwöbel, "Gesetz und Evangelium."
5. For example, Heim, *The Depth of the Riches*; D'Costa, *The Meeting of Religions and the Trinity*; Kärkkäinen, *Trinity and Religious Pluralism*.
6. See the recent discussion at Slenczka, "Texte zum Alten Testament."

7. Voetius, *Selectae disputationes theologicae*, deel IV, 26, 'Iam vero Evangelium stricte dictum, ut à lege distinguitur, directe & per se non praescribit nobis officium nostrum, aut quid nos facere debeamus, dicendo, hoc fac, aut crede, aut confide; [...] Sed refert, nuntiat, significat nobis, quid Christus pro nobis fecerit, quidque Deus in Christo promittat, quid facere velit, & facturus sit.'

## Bibliography

Crisp, O. *Retrieving Doctrine: Essays in Reformed Theology*. Downers Grove, IL: IVP Academic, 2010.

D'Costa, G. *Christian Uniqueness Reconsidered: The Myth of a Pluralistic Theology of Religions*. Maryknoll, NY: Orbis Books, 1990.

D'Costa, G. *The Meeting of Religions and the Trinity*. Maryknoll, NY: Orbis Books, 2000.

Heim, S. M. *The Depth of the Riches: A Trinitarian Theology of Religious Ends*. Grand Rapids, MI: W.B. Eerdmans, 2001.

Kärkkäinen, V.-M. *Trinity and Religious Pluralism: The Doctrine of the Trinity in Christian Theology of Religions*. Burlington, VT: Ashgate, 2004.

Moyaert, M. *Fragile Identities: Towards a Theology of Interreligious Hospitality*. Amsterdam: Rodopi, 2011.

Schwöbel, C. "Gesetz Und Evangelium." In *RGG*, 4th ed., Vol. 3, 862–867. Tübingen: Mohr Siebeck, 1998.

Slenczka, N. "Texte zum Alten Testament – Systematische Theologie/Dogmatik." Geraadpleegd 6 November 2015. https://www.theologie.hu-berlin.de/de/st/AT

Voetius, G. *Selectae Disputationes Theologicae*. Ultrajecti: Johannes à Waesberge, 1648.

Webster, J. "Theologies of Retrieval." In *The Oxford Handbook of Systematic Theology*, edited by K. Tanner, J. Webster, and I. Torrance, 583–599. Oxford: Oxford University Press, 2007.

Wolterstorff, N. "Toleration Justice, and Dignity. Lecture on the Occasion of the Inauguration as Professor of Dirk-Martin Grube, Free University of Amsterdam, September 24, 2015." *International Journal of Philosophy and Theology* 75, no. 5, (2015): 377–386.

# Uncertain musings about the state of the world and religion's contribution

Joseph Margolis

I distinguish between religions of divinity and civilizational religions within the diversity of what I call 'mythic discourse' and explain the difference between agentive and enabling norms applied to the life of persons treated along broadly Darwinian lines as artifactual transforms of the human primate. I consider how to view 'truth' in naturalistic and religious contexts relative to the distinctions mentioned.

This is a special and very happy occasion, honoring Dirk-Martin's installation as the new chair of Religious Diversity and the Epistemology of Theology/Religion, in the Faculty of Theology. I'm more than pleased to join the celebration, which rounds out my first impression of Dirk-Martin's merit when he first began his doctoral studies in the United States a good many years ago.

I am myself something of an interloper in these proceedings and may require a bit of your tolerance even beyond the themes of religious diversity: partly because I take myself to be a Martian visitor not entirely at home with Earth-bound practices and convictions, partly because I'm temperamentally drawn to no more than an extremely thin understanding of what counts as a viable and reasonable reading of genuinely religious concerns, and partly because I find myself to be rather heterodox regarding the main questions of professional philosophy, particularly those that bear on defining the conditions of knowledge and the norms of right conduct, taken in the widest sense. Otherwise, I behave in a perfectly respectable way conversationally and at the dinner table.

I cannot, however, approach the religious question, except confessionally. That's to say: I'm unable to treat divinity in any literalminded way, whether with regard to the Creation of all that is, naturally or supernaturally, or with regard to the revelation of the ultimate norms or obligations of human life. I see no convincing way in which such questions can be met by the straightforward discovery of determinate truths about the world, but I'm not prepared to dismiss them either, as, say, delusive or irrational or meaningless or anything of the sort. What is true or false about the world bears in an important and complex – albeit disputatious – way on the defensibility of pertinent religious beliefs. But I find I must set such beliefs apart as requiring a distinctive form of interpretation, if they are open to validation at all; they concern the perceived meaning and worth of mortal life in a certain personally compelling and absorbing executive sense that people find they need and can sustain – and that sustains them. Some seem to have no need of any such strenuous supports. I may be one of these, though I find myself sympathetically affected by the heavy dependence of others on such beliefs. In any case, though we speak of such beliefs as 'truths,' they cannot be processed in quite the same way standard beliefs are tested.

Call that piety, deemed valid in the most minimal sense, if indeed, individually or societally, we are able and willing, or obliged, to live in accord with such doctrines. Usually, they impose strenuous demands of their own on our lives, not merely of a moral sort; but the bare idea of piety, thus construed, may be, if history is to be trusted, as diverse, extreme, contentious, disputed, idiosyncratic, paradoxical, violently opposed by alternative pieties, unlikely to be universally adopted (as anything one can imagine) – and, of course, potentially dangerous to opposed or alien pieties. Our pieties are valid, then, at least honorifically, in that it seems impossible to demonstrate that there are grounds of validation that are entirely independent of the local convictions of the adherents of opposed such pieties, by which apparent claims can be effectively adjudicated. Our arguments here are largely circular, though that is not to say that it would be unreasonable to propose further constraints of some consensual sort in order to facilitate a measure of compatibility among otherwise regionally opposed such pieties.

Still, no such accommodation can be counted on to disqualify (convincingly) the minimal validity of exclusionary claims, however exotic or extreme. In our time, for instance, we cannot fail to acknowledge, at least secretly, that the great monotheisms have, over an immensity of time, often claimed exclusive, even brutally violent rights of validity with regard to alternative forms of piety. The entire Middle East is now absorbed in such a contest. As a Martian, I'm bound to say that war to the bitter end is not in any obvious regard incompatible with the most heartfelt and sublime piety. I think, for instance, of the crusade against the Albigenians. Piety is not any assurance of political peace: and peace may be no more than a temporary and partisan objective, whereas the most intense pieties may be served by unconditional war. We need a better picture of what may be rightly claimed, here, in the way of truth and validity.

In effect, I'm suggesting that even the minimal definition of religious piety may not be separable from the question of the objective validity of what to count as a 'true' form of piety itself; also, that the resolution of the matter may well – I think it must – betray the profound circularity of the entire issue. I concede that a tolerance of religious diversity is an attractive idea – a notable accomplishment of the Netherlands for instance – but I am not prepared to pronounce such a conviction an assured moral or religious or civilizational truth that can be straightforwardly validated, or validated on other grounds in such a way that to oppose it renders the opposed claim patently invalid.

I don't think the intended demonstration gains any force at all by being addressed under the auspices of 'truth' adjusted to the special inquiries of religion or of any laxer notion of 'validity' exceeding the narrower constraints of truth. Both maneuvers presume to have some rule of normative privilege in their back pocket. For convenience, though with due regard to the peculiarities of religious inquiry, I suggest we collect these matters as falling within the space of what may be called 'mythic discourse,' since what we take to be true or valid in the religious sense tends to address the would-be disclosures of some divinity or Creator of the totality of all there is, or of the ultimate concerns of human life, or some other extreme condition of this sort, that cannot normally be explored by familiar procedures of practical Earth-bound life. I have suggestions to offer about how these matters may be usefully examined in our time, now that we have formed a palpable sense of global propinquity and technological power affecting all of globalized life, that makes the very question of species survival an unavoidable issue for the whole of mankind. Here, religion shows a definite need to consider historical adjustment: as with such matters as abortion, assisted suicide, same-sex marriage and the like. There seem to be no changeless or incontestable human objectives of this gauge and no plausible ground for a disjunction of religious and moral/political validation.

Let me intrude, then, two very general constraints that apply to disputes regarding defensible forms of piety as well as science and practical life (without further distinction) that strongly suggest the rational relevance of ordinary truth-claims with regard to the defensibility of would-be religious doctrines open, one way or another, to interpretation along what I shall call mythic lines (as just bruited) I should say at once that I don't regard mythic thinking as mere fiction or falsehood. I take it to be a very reasonable conjecture (all but certainly true) that holds that the evolution of our species, Homo sapiens sapiens, along broadly Darwinian and post-Darwinian lines (hence, both biologically and culturally), is unique in such a way that, on the best biological and linguistically qualified cultural grounds, neither the human primate nor the human person (distinguished in a way that must be spelled out) can be shown to occupy a determinate ecological or teleological role or niche or function or purpose, in terms of which the objectives of would-be religiously responsible life may be said to be straightforwardly discovered.

On naturalistic grounds, to the best approximation, the human being has no discernible place in nature or the universe at large by which to guide or govern pieties. I shall make this a bit clearer in a moment. But the point at stake is simply that a convincing case can easily be made to demonstrate that, confined to truth-claims about the natural world, the formulation of ultimate human purposes governing how we should live our lives – what I shall call 'agentive norms' – the target of Kant's Categorical Imperative, for instance – cannot be more than artifactual posits of our enlanguaged and encultured Bildung.

What I propose here is that the human being has no natural grounds on which to determine its place or purpose or noblest objectives within the constraints of natural and mortal life – a fortiori, within the terms of piety itself. Wherever it posits moral, political, educational, or religious goals, it invokes a mythic vision of some sort: where, we may say, the difference between the political and the religious tends to disappear or requires some sort of naturalized interpretation, in order to bring one's ordinary pieties to bear on the details of mundane life.

That humans have no assignable place in nature is, I argue, a true consequence of the evolution of the human – as in witnessing a birth or death. I take it to depend on the conceptual distinction between the human primate and the human person.

I myself believe that the invention of true language (unique, as far as we know, to humans) and the transformation of the human primate into a person (by way of the mastery of language, beginning in infancy) are obverse sides of one and the same process. So that, in my idiom, persons are historied, enlanguaged, hybrid artifacts of a unique form of evolution peculiar to the human species, creatures that, by mastering language, are effectively capacitated to invent acceptably encompassing objectives for their own lives. Being reflective (because enlanguaged), they require, if they are to survive, steady, convincing purposes in a purposeless world. Religion may be the single most impressive source of inspiration for the invention of suitable agentive norms. I take this to be a positive feature of mythic imagination, which, in a way, both Marx and Freud ignore.

The ultimate fragility of human purposes, particularly in our warlike, wasteful, confused, unruly world, suggests the importance of sustainable practices of communal piety – and even yields clues about the relative advantages and disadvantages of alternative convictions. I'm suggesting that piety has indeed a rational, thoroughly artifactual function in any human economy, that can be assessed in perfectly mundane ways. (I'll come back to that.)

In any case, the analysis of what it is to be a person may well be the single most important philosophical question that we ever address. For, if I'm right in treating persons as hybrid, artifactual, enlanguaged transforms of human primates (effectively, human infants), then even the analysis of science and rational conduct – hence, questions of truth and validation – must be dependent on the contingent varieties of historied life. This begins to make sense of the profound diversity of the forms of human life and the penetrative powers of piety. But it also leads me to the second of the two preliminary premises I've promised: namely, that it is impossible to discover (in any sense akin to what we mean by practical know-how or science) the true norms of agentive life, especially the putatively noblest or most ultimate and consequential that we find ourselves willing to tender under cover of religious piety.

In the dialogue known as Statesman, Plato offers what appears to be a joke at the expense of his greatest dialogue, the Republic, to the effect that man is a herd animal that must govern itself by suitable laws, though it lacks the barest ability to discover such laws: a giant step well in advance of Nietzsche. I take this (second) truth about the human condition to be directly derivable from the first – or to be tantamount to it: so that, as a consequence, all human efforts to formulate an acceptable set of agentive norms for the needs of mundane life, as well as piety, must themselves be artifactual posits, 'second-best' (as we may say), on the strength of the premise that there is no pertinent form of natural discovery to appeal to.

On the evidence of physics and astronomy, we are born into an uncomprehending and indifferent world – and must invent the ultimate purposes that we find adequate to live by. What is intriguing about this requirement is that the validity of such inventions is itself an artifact, a construct, of our curious evolution: precisely, an artifact of the artifactual invention of natural language itself within the continuum of the communicative powers of languageless animals, in accord with which, as an unavoidable byproduct, we become aware of the fateful isolation of our species – and act, spontaneously, to remedy the matter. The story I'm telling is itself a low-grade bit of mythic thinking that a grander speculation might succor. Here, also, we arrive at a reasonable simplification from which to launch a plausible theory of the logic of religion itself and of what passes for truth and validation among competing claims. But there's much that's still missing here that must be filled in, if we are ever to come to a generous and convincing analysis and resolution of the conundrum. I have two further theorems to offer – and then a speculation about the logic of religious beliefs that will return us to Dirk-Martin's own account of the grounds for favoring a policy of 'religious diversity.' I'll close with that.

The first of these last two theorems, that is, the third of my proposals, is essentially a verbal matter that clarifies the 'logic' of agentive norms, with regard to truth and validation. I suggest that, essentially, there are two kinds of norms we live by: what may be called 'agentive' and 'enabling' norms. The distinction is a functional one: the same norms may function in either role. Though if they do, they are obliged to play by different rules, respectively. For example, health may be both an agentive and an enabling norm. It's a logical feature of enabling norms that they may be paraphrased acceptably by non-normative formulations (causal or instrumental or inferential or interpretive or the like) in ways that may be straightforwardly confirmed as true or false. Thus, regardless of one's agentive purpose, if improved health is an enabling consideration in ensuring agentive success, then a causal paraphrase (say, nutritional or clinical) will be bound to serve; and valuational issues may then be treated in straight-forwardly truth-bearing ways. But agentive norms, especially those that appear among our noblest or most ultimate and encompassing norms – options that may invoke a supporting piety – cannot be confirmed by any merely paraphrastic means of the enabling sort. There's where normativity of the agentive kind joins hands with the logic of religious piety.

We cannot in any sense discern the right norms of human life: we are simply drawn to those we favor or oppose and we change our loyalties with changing experience, maturity, conviction, argument, the habits of life of our home society, accessibility to enabling norms, and the like. Here, I suggest a useful vocabulary. Because, in mastering the natural language we begin to acquire in infancy and the cultural resources that such mastery subtends, it begins to dawn on us that we are 'always already' furnished with an incipient grasp of the agentive and enabling norms of our own tribe. We are never confronted with the need to invent, from scratch, the norms that we are prepared to live by. We are never so deprived: we couldn't be. Furthermore, whatever changes we propose among our agentive norms (vouchsafed, as I've suggested, in accord with the mythic powers of our society's effective form of piety) tend to be reconciled with a suitably adjusted form of piety itself. I think here of the Afghan Taliban's policy of decapitating young girls committed to gaining a formal education and the speed with which same-sex marriage was approved in the United States after pronouncements of support by the President and Vice-President of the country.

In some societies, of course, same-sex marriage is a theological matter; but then, you must take note of the fact that a radically altered consensus of piety may be instantly formed, under hospitable circumstances, without benefit of clergy, so to say. The same, it has been argued, momentously occurred in the reign of Amenhotep IV, in the fourteenth century B.C., in Egypt, affecting the reconstruction of the supposed role of the Egyptian Moses in the first formulations of the great monotheisms of the Middle East, eclipsing what have been called polytheisms and cosmotheisms, which tend to confirm the natural intertwinement of mythic and rational debate about the merits of religious innovation. (I shall come back to an important aspect of such changes.)

But what I offer here is simply a bit of convenient vocabulary to help us collect the rest of my tale.

I want to say that our quotidian norms, whether agentive or enabling, that we discover are 'always already' in play, as we master out language and culture from infancy on, are, borrowing loosely from Hegel's usage, 'sittlich,' meaning by that that such norms are no more than customary, operatively effective, relatively uncontested, essentially prescriptive, open to revision and change in consensual ways that may themselves acquire sittlich standing. It matters little, 'logically,' whether we say that the doctrines we draw from such practices are 'true' or 'valid' or what have you. (William James seems to have been too anxious or too opportunistic here: the issue is no more than honorific.) We acquire our pieties in the same way we acquire our home language. As far as I'm concerned, there is no logical route by which to establish the right norms of agentive life, except on internal grounds. But that does not mean that, once given in the sittlich way, there are no rational, 'second-best' reasons for revising our pieties as well as our agentive norms.

There's the radical import of the simplification I recommend. Every society looks to itself for evidence of changes of consensual conviction regarding the prevailing forms of piety and agentive norms at least: enlarge the meaning of religious, political, educative, moral, historical sensibilities, and you enlarge the innovative possibilities of sittlich life itself. I therefore borrow from Rousseau, to mark the lesson, the admittedly problematic notion of a discernible change in the collective conviction of a tribe or people (what Rousseau calls the collective 'will of all' (la volonté générale), that cannot rightly be quantified and cannot rightly be demonstrated to have obtained – but which societies presume to discern from time to time – and are thus justified to act on.

The idea that we can go further, confirmationally, is more than problematic. Ultimately, I may as well confess, even the attribution of truth and knowledge in the sciences rests to some extent on circular, self-serving grounds. The marvel is that that sort of skeptical tolerance is entirely compatible with the compelling achievement of the sciences and practical skills we claim to exert. Once we abandon the pretenses of cognitive privilege, we cannot validate (except vacuously) the competence such apparent success is said to presuppose. We cannot demonstrate that what we suppose we've come to know, we assuredly know; or that, in understanding the meaning of what we say, we understand, confirmationally, what it is to understand such meanings. The only answer we can possibly give betrays our confidence in the reliability of cultural immersion itself – but that's hardly an argument. I cannot see that the validation of piety draws on stronger grounds. Here, we simply learn that we are at the limit of our explanatory resources. If we say that we must fall back, even here, to the resources of piety, I should protest that we've deceived ourselves. The self-referential paradoxes are not themselves a source of productive knowledge. And neither is piety. But, if so, then no one should object if we pronounce our verdict a form of wisdom. I'm not persuaded that we need a novel logic here.

The second theorem of my second sort (that is, my fourth proposal) introduces a heterodox distinction between very different kinds of religions: apart from standard (admittedly important) distinctions between polytheisms, cosmotheisms, and monotheisms, and the like (or, indeed, between theisms and deisms), I think it useful to distinguish between religions centered on the worship or contemplation of, or analogous engagements with, deities or divinities that, whether exoterically or esoterically, may be addressed in essentially personal terms ('theistic religions,' in the broadest sense), and what I name (perhaps arbitrarily) 'civilizational religions,' religions that feature forms of piety addressed, agentively, to matters of 'ultimate concern' or 'the totality of all that is,' but that exclude all personal relationships involving divinities as irrelevant or misleading or committed to false beliefs, if intended in some literal sense of truth and falsity shared with inquiries like those of the sciences.

These categories are intended merely as a matter of classificatory convenience: it's entirely possible that historical religions may involve a mixture of the theistic and the civilizational. Perhaps Confucianism, Daoism, early Buddhism, Stoicism, Epicureanism, and Spinozism may be regarded as fair specimens of the civilizational sort and the great monotheisms, obvious specimens of the theistic sort. But the incompletely resolved complexities of the supposed Mosaic contribution involving the relationship between Egyptian and Hebraic conceptions of divinity have raised the possibility that the origins of the Abrahamic monotheisms may lie in some more complex amalgam in which even what I'm calling the theistic and the civilizational may be conceptually united and reconciled.

On my view, both sorts of religion or piety require the admission of what I've called mythic discourse: the theistic, because a literal reading of divinity cannot be reconciled with any purely naturalistic restrictions on what to count as belonging to 'what there is'; the civilizational, because ultimate (agentive) concerns and the totality of all that there is are not, in any ordinary sense, accessible to inquiries that yield truths or truth-bearing claims of a practical sort.

Viewed informally, theistic religions strongly favor the primacy of a mythic idiom, though it is entirely possible that true believers intend their devotions in some literal way, even where practice cannot fail to generate insoluble paradoxes and the threat of irrationality; civilizational religions tend to favor rational and naturalized belief, though their characteristic concerns, ultimate or unconditional objectives and attention to the totality of all that is, normally exceed the familiar competences of ordinary inquiry and risk the intimacy of personalized relations with the abstract divinity of the whole. Aggregated, regular demonstrations of piety tend to favor the theistic mode; individual contemplation tends to favor the interpreted coherence of holistic civilizational belief.

The theistic tends to erase the difference between religion and politics (as with the principal monotheisms); the civilizational tends to feature cosmological coherence, hence, also, the solution of problems of local order in terms of the conceptual unity of the cosmos itself. Each extreme tends to coopt and distance the advantages and disadvantages of its opposite. The history of religion tends to favor cosmic simplicity, as political life tends to become globalized; but religious effectivity tends to take a political or practical form: hence, favors local divinities. In this sense, both modes tend to treat religion increasingly as a form of notably elevated agentive commitment, whether ethical or contemplative, and each coopts the supplementary strength of the other.

I see no reason to object to theistic claims that declare, for instance, that, as with the original Hebrews, circumcision is, 'in truth' a condition of ritual cleanliness rather than, say, a medicinal or hygienic matter, whether or not a Freudian explanation is forthcoming. But there may be a conflict between natural and medical or hygienic (or related) concerns; and, there, the dispute cannot be construed, naturalistically or rationally, as a conflict of confirmable truths, in any sense of truth said to be unequivocally shared with the sciences and practical life.

In this sense, mythic 'truths' cannot fail to be open to rational challenge (under the condition of pertinent interpretation), without requiring the revision of any canonical account of truth itself. There may well be compelling reasons for favoring the 'truths of piety' over the 'truths of science,' but not (convincingly) at the price of changing our conception of truth in investigating nature or of introducing a system of dual concepts or criteria of truth (that must then be continually adjudicated, case by case).

It's also a very natural conjecture that holds that wherever the civilizational displaces the theistic or diminishes its prescriptive authority, the requirements of ritual piety are, when collisions with naturalistically grounded norms come into play (medicinal or political, for instance); likely to yield to agentive norms thought to be 'rational' on independent grounds (equal justice for all, say) or collectively entrenched under pertinent historical circumstances (slavery, same-sex marriage, female circumcision). Here, again, there's no need to fiddle with any reasonably workable canon of truth.

But puzzles of a deeper and very different sort arise when, say, we consider a pronouncement like 'God is unfathomable.' I don't think this can be read in the same manner in which Kant, for instance, speaks of what is real utterly without reference to human inquiry (the infamous Ding-an-sich), simply because, read as a theorem of negative theology, we do indeed 'fathom' God well enough to know that He is 'unfathomable'! Here, 'unfathomable' is a substantive predicate of mythic discourse about the natural world. It is not a viable predicate within Kantian philosophy, for instance, or within Kant's rational theology; and it is not a deviant or supplementary truth-value or truth-like value of any kind. Its use is indeed parasitic on what is said to be 'fathomed' in some antecedent mythic mode ('revealed' by a divine source, for instance, because, as with Nicholas of Cusa, human cognitive faculties are admitted to be inadequate to the task). Similarly, if one says that God's mode of being is 'indetermi-nate,' 'indeterminate' is not (or at least need not be) a 'truth-value' of any kind: I'd say it was a second-order predicate that signified that we cannot address the question of God's mode of being by procedures suited to determining the nature or mode of being of anything in the natural world. That's all. It's here that we turn to the supposed resources of mythic discourse. If the Trinity is a 'mystery,' then what we probably mean to say is that we cannot explain (in any naturalistic way) how God's unity can be manifested in terms of the putative integrity of determinably distinct persons. Nevertheless, I have myself been acquainted with at least one logician (the American logician, Richard Martin), who was convinced that he could demonstrate the formal coherence of the Trinitarian doctrine, in accord with its apparent religious sense.

No. These questions (those just considered) do not touch at all on the matter of 'religious diversity,' that is, on possible ways in which the validation of diverse beliefs (if I understand the matter at all) may affect our account of truth and validation, the question that occupies Dirk-Martin at the present time. I see no reason to think that the 'logical' question is peculiar to issues like that of religious diversity (as, say, opposed to moral diversity), and I don't think Dirk-Martin thinks it is either. The best way to proceed, as I see the matter, is to offer an analogue of skeptically religious application. I have always found abundant examples in political, moral, historical, legal, and art-critical contexts. They all belong to the enlanguaged world of human culture, a world of Intentionality and the interpretation of meanings and normative standing. Logically, the question remains whether a conventional bivalent logic can accommodate our practice in different domains and inquiries adequately. Many subtle questions arise here, of course. But we need only select a few. For instance, I'm persuaded that it would be a mistake to displace bivalence altogether – say, with some schema of many-valued truth-values, in order to support (what I at least would call) relativistic claims, judgments, assertions, or the like.

Dirk-Martin is quite right to emphasize that the need for an alternative array of truth-values or truth-like values arises wherever we are prepared to defend 'beliefs' or (what I call) 'agentive commitments' as 'valid' in whatever sense we concede is suitably analogous to confirming the 'truth' of ordinary assertions – but would generate unwanted paradoxes, if not suitably enabled. As long as we are able to treat bivalent logic (with due restrictions of scope) as compatible, formally, with the use of a many-valued logic that supersedes bivalence in the restricted range conceded) – even if applied ad hoc to individual cases of a kind that, for suitable reasons, we wish to protect or enable – there is no need to assign our strategy, antecedently, to any special domain of cases before we apply the supplementary schema. We can apply the schema ad hoc. The matter is quite straightforward. We seek no more than a plausible strategy (a logical gimmick, really), for admitting as valid, sets of paired assertions, judgments, propositions, beliefs, claims, commitments thought to yield paraphrastic equivalents of the kinds just mentioned, that, in accord with a bivalent logic but not now (that is, in accord with our laxer schema), would be deemed to take on incompatible and opposed truth-values.

Imagine for instance, that we ask for a valid historical account of World War I and are offered two very detailed accounts that overlap considerably in what they claim, include a small number of claims one of our paired accounts does not mention, fail to include some that one mate includes – some of both of which appear to be reasonably supported within the account in which they appear and yet would be reasonably opposed if they are mentioned in the account in which they do not appear. Imagine that when we examine the two accounts separately, without reference to the other, we are reasonably convinced (as competent historians) that each account has featured, without distortion or the like, adequate important factors in a coherent way; that each account might easily have been deemed a true account of what happened; and that, nevertheless, when we bring the two together, we cannot find sufficient grounds to treat the apparent incompatibilities bivalently. We are tempted to say that both are reasonably valid but we cannot say that both are strictly true (on pain of contradiction).

So we agree that both are reasonable or plausible or apt or the like, well on the way to being counted as true, except that we cannot in good conscience disallow the comparable standing of its opposed mate. We therefore restrict the use of the rule of excluded middle and the rule of tertium non datur for the case at hand. I would say we've fallen back to the liberties of a relativistic logic, not merely a many-valued logic (a probability logic, for instance), because we have explicitly allowed restrictions of logical scope (ad hoc) in the manner sketched. Many are worried by the use of the term 'relativistic' here. But, of course, I've set important constraints on its usage. Surely, in many circumstances, including beliefs that concern matters of 'religious diversity,' we are willing to adopt such a strategy.

Furthermore, we've made allowances of a noticeably informal sort, which we might defend in terms of the distinctive nature of the claims we tender. If anyone wishes to speak of religious beliefs (of the sort examined) as being 'true,' we have only to remind ourselves that we are speaking of 'claims' and 'assertions' in the mythic mode, that is, claims and assertions that require interpretation of a difficult sort in order to determine the fit of such claims with the usual range of claims that invite standard ascriptions of truth. When, in accord with Old Testament tradition, one examines the validity of the prohibition 'not to seethe the kid in his mother's milk,' we must consider that, though it expresses a very nice scruple, times may have changed so drastically that to regard the rule as unconditionally inviolable now may simply be too rigid for our altered sensibilities. What was once forbidden may now be deemed permissible, with due care. I cannot see the logical difference between this case and the case of same-sex marriage, once we concede that persons are artifacts of enlanguaged culture. But, of course, if you admit this much, you will have gone a considerable distance in allowing that religious beliefs may be as profoundly subject to historical revision along lines that cannot, now, disqualify the relevance of naturalistic practices of determining such truths. Is it too vile a thought to suggest that the Biblical account of Sodom and Gomorrah has lost a great deal of its force as far as the validation of a homosexual life style is concerned?

We've come full circle now. For, if we cannot deny the bearing of history on the validity of religious beliefs, then, on the strength of the argument offered, we cannot escape the sittlich forces that influence our new projections. And if that's true, then religious diversity is much the same, logically, as political, economic, legal, artistic, and moral diversity; and, there, there are no timeless rules to draw on. We may even be tempted to concede that, with regard to agentive norms, there is no fundamental difference between confirming religious and moral and political truths or regarding the scope and relevance of mythic discourse. And, of course, beyond religious diversity, there looms the question of the sheer tolerance of human sensibilities, the limits of which we cannot claim to know.

# Tolerance and religious belief: a response to Joseph Margolis

## Oliver J. Wiertz

I offer a reconstruction of J. Margolis' article on the question of the meaning and place of religion in our time proposing that one of its main subjects is the question of religious tolerance. I hint at the possible gains of a religiously less attenuated picture of religious belief than that which Margolis paints.

Professor Margolis has undertaken the demanding task of wrestling with the question of the meaning and place of religion in our time and the question of religious tolerance, paying due tribute to the contemporary culture with its own conditions and standards of comprehensibility and rationality, but also paying due tribute to the genuine resources of religion and respecting its integrity – even if he is not able to affirm anything more than 'an extremely thin understanding of … genuinely religious concerns' (407).

In the following, I am mainly trying to give my own reconstruction of some of Margolis' main topics and then hint at two points where perhaps a little less thin understanding of religious concerns can back his plea for a skeptical tolerance, which I view as one of the cores of his paper. It goes without saying that I cannot do justice to his rich and complex paper but I will at least pick out some topics.

In my view, Margolis' case rests on two pillars.

The first is the acceptance of the fact that it is not rationally feasible to reflect on religious and anthropological questions in our time without acknowledging the findings of the sciences. In this sense, but only in this wide sense, Margolis proposes a naturalistic stance. And that leads to the second pillar.

Evolution theory has taught us that we do not occupy a special place or play a determinate role in a universe which is in fact indifferent about our well-being. We have to face the demanding task of living in a world without purposes. We have no natural resources to find a definite place or role but must construct our place in the cosmos and the meaning of our life by ourselves. We are urged to make them up on our own and especially on our own risk I would add.

The same goes for the true norms of morality. Margolis affirms the impossibility of discovering the true norms of 'Sittlichkeit.' Instead of getting to know them we have to construct the deepest principles and norms of 'Sittlichkeit' ourselves. The norms of morality are constructed and so are the tests for their validity. But the task of constructing our moral norms and principles is a difficult one, as is likewise our appreciation of intrinsic values, e.g., the intrinsic dignity and worth of human beings (in Margolis

35

terminology: our agentive norms), that is constantly threatened by instrumental rationality, so-called 'Zweck-Mittel Rationalität,' which is said to have a purely non-normative foundation, and therefore cannot do justice to so-called agentive norms. But agentive norms cannot and should not be reduced to enabling norms.

That is Margolis' picture of the conditio humana, highlighting our all-encompassing frailty.

At this point, religion or piety enters into the picture because religion is an important source for purposes and meaning and it is a potential ally for agentive norms or at least it shares with those a kind of logic which cannot be translated into the idiom of instrumental rationality.

Margolis understands piety as the willingness and ability to live in accord with religious doctrines that could be counted as answers to the existential and ethical questions mentioned before. Margolis is anxious to stress that these doctrines should not be understood literally but rather taken as mythical truths. It is easier to say what he does not mean by mythical than to give a positive account. One thing seems clear: He does not equate mythical with fictional or delusional. His allusion to the mythical character of piety has nothing in common with the 'delusion talk' offered by some critics of religion.[1] A clue to the positive meaning of Margolis' concept of myth is the way of dealing with ultimate concerns of our life within religions, as a consequence of which religious doctrines cannot be dealt with like scientific hypotheses or questions of daily life.

But now things get complicated and at times even dramatic because there are many different forms of piety so that no single form could be universally adopted (although at least some of them claim universal acceptance and are therefore dangerous for other forms of piety). The effects of religious differences are the more dramatic as the different forms of piety cannot be validated in a universalistic way, in which all rational people would come to more or less identical conclusions. That this is not only of theoretical interest is shown by the history of the great monotheistic religions. It is a sad lesson we have to learn in realizing that 'war to the bitter end' is not in any way incompatible with deep und even sublime piety. But all that does not mean that there are not any arguments or reasons at all in the area of religious belief – but rather that they are all largely circular. And even if one adds further requirements one cannot level a convincing critique against exclusionary claims – not even against the extreme ones.

An often pursued way to circumvent these problems is to separate religious questions totally from questions of truth and validation. Because, so the hope, if the different religions relinquish their opposing truth claims and validation practices there would not be any reason for violent conflicts between them any longer. The differences between religions will loose their bitterness and will become in the end more or less irrelevant – at least for those in the society who are not interested in religious doctrines or practices.

But Margolis does not choose this option – rightly as I would say. But now he faces a dilemma: On the one hand he thinks that even a minimal understanding of piety cannot do without truth – because every respectable form of piety must face the task of distinguishing between true and untrue forms of piety. Yet religious truth claims are viewed by many as a source of dangerous threats to peace in general and to liberal societies in particular. But on the other hand there is not any possibility of a noncircular validation of religious claims. And such a possibility seems to be indispensable for preventing a violent unfolding of religious differences and for fostering a civilized, rational way of dealing with these questions – as, for example, John Locke intended to do.

That leads to the next uncomfortable problem. Though Margolis seems to sympathize with the idea of tolerance, even that idea cannot be justified as a fundamental truth, binding all human beings and functioning as an arbiter of all religious claims. But, so my interpretation: if the intellectual foundation of tolerance is not as certain as some have thought, religious fanatics (as well as secularist fanatics) would not have any problem to abandon the idea of toleration in theory and in practice. This diagnosis gets an even more dramatic tone if one agrees with Margolis' suggestion that the theistic version of piety tends 'to erase the difference between religion and politics' (403). That frightening outlook should call on us to the search for a better understanding of truth and validity in the religious area.

I recommend that we should view Margolis as suggesting two moves towards a better understanding.

The first move is to stress the historical and constructive character of every form of religion. A contemporary credible form of piety has to acknowledge its deeply historical and constructive character. It cannot draw on neutral grounds beyond all particular communities or practices but has to rest content with merely internal kinds of justification. But all this means neither that piety is to be denigrated (even sciences rest at least to some extent on internal, i.e., circular grounds) nor does it mean that religion is in the clear, i.e., invulnerable to any rational critique. This is prohibited by Margolis' two first constraints, which bring back ordinary truth claims into the field.[2] In one sentence: religions have to acknowledge their contingent character and should draw their lessons from this acknowledgement. So, Margolis encourages moral and religious communities to look beyond their borders to stimulate their imagination and push forward ethical or religious innovations.

Margolis' epistemically rather weak picture in combination with this advice grounds a 'skeptical tolerance' (which is nonetheless compatible with the achievements of science and the development of our practical skills).

This skeptical tolerance is further strengthened by his second move: the ad hoc restriction of the principle of bivalence, i.e., the principle that every assertive sentence/ proposition has just one of exactly two possible truth values: true or false. Every proposition, e.g., that Amsterdam has more than five inhabitants, must be either true or false. And therefore, if the proposition is not false, it must be true. What does this have to do with the problem of religious diversity? From the principle of bivalence, it follows first that there is no proposition which is neither true nor false and second that if you view a proposition not as true you must view it as false. So, if a believer, call him Michael, meets a follower of some other tradition of piety, call her Susan, and Susan talks to Michael about her faith, e.g., that she believes that God is three persons in one divine nature, but Michael believes that there is not only one divine nature but also only one divine person, Michael has to view Susan's belief in the trinity as not true and therefore as false. At least as far as the principle of bivalence goes. But what should Michael do if he views his own strictly monotheistic belief as rational and backed by some reasons and on the other hand has to acknowledge that also Susan has good reasons for her belief? If he had not held a strict monotheistic belief before meeting her, he would perhaps have become a Trinitarian theist due to the reasons she gave him for her belief. Michael cannot view both his belief and Susan's Trinitarian belief as true in the strict sense, because that would be a contradiction and even if Margolis is a heretic in philosophy he seems to be reluctant to become an arch-heretic abandoning the law of non-contradiction, according to which the propositions p and non-p cannot both be true.

Margolis would admonish Susan and Michael to take the epistemic credentials of both propositions seriously. And therefore, he suggests ad hoc restrictions of the bivalence principle, taking both contradictory propositions as reasonably valid or rational but not as true in the strict sense but being 'on the right way to truth,' a phrase which sounds familiar to those dealing with the problem of religious plurality in theology or philosophy.[3]

All this leads to an attenuated picture of religious truth claims or truth claims of any kind in the service of a skeptical tolerance.

In spite of the prima facie attractiveness of Margolis's reconstruction of religious belief, two concluding remarks shall point out the resources of an epistemologically less attenuated picture of religious belief:

Obviously, Margolis sees evolution theory as leading inevitably to a view of human beings as higher animals with no definite special place in the natural sphere. Margolis does not seem to be entirely satisfied with his conclusion. This lack of uniqueness and a stable place on the part of the human species seems to endanger our moral dignity because there is the constant threat of viewing humans solely under the perspective of instrumental rationality. But such a view cannot do justice to the intrinsic value of every human being as it is formulated in the humanity-formula of Kant's categorical imperative.[4] Let me hint at a possible solution. Let us grant Margolis, for the sake of the argument, his premise that we are artefactual persons and therefore have to construct ourselves as well as our purposes and norms. But we as human beings are the only species in a position to create itself. Or to say it in another way: we belong to the only species that was able to develop a language sufficient for discursive aims, especially for normative discourses. At least this makes us special. If we have no special place naturally, we have at least created a special place for us and thereby have made ourselves special beings. But this capacity to make ourselves special is itself natural and a characteristic of our species which raises us above all other species and therefore shows that we indeed have a special place. And if the outmoded theistic metaphysics, that I still view as a viable alternative to naturalistic worldviews, is right then this special status is not merely a product of chance or of our own ingenuity but a product of an eternal source of being and of the invincible love of this source for us frail beings. If there is such a loving source of being we do not have to worry that the narrative of our lives will be left unfinished for all times and that our dignity will be threatened in many ways and ultimately destroyed. I have to admit, that I mean these claims literally (and furthermore, that I believe that there are rational reasons for such metaphysical claims). And I also have to admit, that I acknowledge and deeply esteem human freedom. And I would like to think that I do the latter not in spite of the former but because of the former, because of a belief in a transcendent being. Perhaps such an old fashioned metaphysical kind of religious faith and theology can even provide a more solid basis for tolerance than the admirable but perhaps a little bit shaky kind of tolerance Margolis refers to. At least his plea for tolerance can be strengthened by such appeals.

At some points, I have wondered whether the devout believer can accept Margolis proposals and I admit that I am not totally convinced that this will work. The reason for my doubts is not that religious beliefs should be shielded off from every rational critique but I wonder if there is a possibility to convince the believer that her own religious tradition leads to or perhaps even demands such a rational scrutiny of that same tradition. Accordingly, I ask myself if one can give reasons for religious tolerance internal to religious traditions. In my opinion one can find resources for such a project in all three monotheistic religions because they all heed the picture of God as a supremely perfect being and creator of the world – a divine being which cannot be exhaustively comprehended by any human being: Deus semper maior est. This special metaphysical status of God can work as a rational criterion, by which the concrete beliefs and the devotional and political praxis within a certain tradition of piety could be judged. I do not think that such metaphysical thoughts can prevent fundamentalism and fanaticism – but they can show the believer a way of adjusting her own concrete practice of piety, how it can be attuned even more to the nature of God, and they can show how her piety could become closer connected to other aspects of her life, especially to her cognitive faculties, and to the society she lives in.

## Notes

1. E.g., Dawkins, *God Delusion*; also compare the title of the second chapter of Stenger, *New Atheism: The Folly of Faith.*
2. By the way, that shows that piety cannot work as a shelter for our limited cognitive capacities, nor as a kind of draw back position in avoiding the threat posed by relativism. Not even on the face of Margolis' robust relativism this would be a viable strategy: a relativism which "admits some range of competing claims, claims for which there are at least minimal grounds justifying the joint application of competing principles"; Margolis, "Robust Relativism," 37.
3. As far as I can see, a common reason for the restriction of the principle of bivalence is the existence of semantic or ontological vagueness. This fits nicely with Margolis' proposal of a mythic understanding of religious discourse which can function as a reason for thinking of religious discourse as vague, which in turns justifies the restriction of the principle of bivalence in the area of religious discourse. For a critique of the use of vagueness as a basis for the rejection of bivalence, see Williamson, Vagueness. Williamson argues, that the vagueness of an assertive sentence does not consist of the semantic fact that neither the predicate nor its negation apply to the subject but of the epistemological fact that we do not know what the case is with the predicate or its negation. With other words: Williamson proposes that "vagueness is a kind of ignorance." (Williamson Vagueness, 145.) His main argument against the denial of the principle of bivalence for certain sentences (not against its total rejection) is that the denial of bivalence for a particular sentence leads to an apparent contradiction because the 'denial of bivalence for a sentence is equivalent to the denial that either it or its negation is true' (145), which leads to the contradictory conclusion that this sentence is both true and not true. If Williamson is right (which I have to admit would be controversial), the strategy to deny the principle of bivalence only for particular sentences (e.g., sentences on which adherents of different religions disagree) would not work.
4. Kant, *Grundlegung*, 429: 'So act that you use humanity, whether in your own person or in the person of any other, always at the same time as an end, never merely as a means.' (Groundwork of the Metaphysics of Morals; edited and translated by M.J. Gregor).

## Bibliography

Dawkins, R. *The God Delusion*. London: Bantam Press, 2006.

Kant, I. *Grundlegung zur Metaphysik der Sitten*. Riga: Hartknoch, 1786.

Margolis, J. "Robust Relativism." *The Journal of Aesthetics and Art Criticism* 35 (1976): 37–46. doi:10.2307/430843.

Margolis, J. "Uncertain Musings about the State of the World and Religion's Contribution." *International Journal of Philosophy and Theology* 76, no. 5 (2015): 397–406.

Stenger, V. *The New Atheism. Taking a Stand for Science and Religion*. Amherst: Prometheus Press, 2009.

Williamson, T. "Vagueness and Ignorance." *Proceedings of the Aristotelian Society* 66 (1992): 145—162.

# 'What's a nice girl like you doing in a place like this?' or 'What's a feminist practical theologian doing amongst a bunch of distinguished philosophers?' A riff on Professor Joe Margolis' paper

Nicola Slee

Rather than offer a detailed or close reading of Margolis' paper, I 'riff' on some key motifs and themes from his paper from the perspective of a feminist practical theologian. I highlight affective and moral dimensions of the experience of engaging with difference, as exemplified in my own experience as a non-philosopher of engaging with a difficult philosophical text, before going on to nuance and add depth to the notion of religious diversity via multidimensional models of faith. I call on feminist and ordinary believers' approaches to inter-religious encounter to illuminate my central concern, namely to root philosophical discourse on pluralism within lived experience, particularly the lived experience of women of faith.

## Introduction

Professor Margolis begins his paper with the admission of being 'something of an interloper in the proceedings' (397). As a stray feminist practical theologian amongst a distinguished body of philosophers, I share something of the status of an outsider. As an interloper into the discussion, there is the risk of saying something wholly inappropriate, missing the mark altogether. On the other hand, the interloper may see things others miss, precisely because, not in spite of, their hermeneutical innocence and unknowing. Therefore, I shall not attempt to play the philosophers at their own game. Neither will I offer a close or detailed reading of Margolis' paper – something I am not equipped to do. Rather, I will endeavour to come at the topic of religious diversity and Professor Margolis' paper, precisely as an outsider to the philosophers' discourse (though recognizing some of their language and concerns). I write as a feminist practical theologian and will attempt to exploit that stance to advantage, contributing a fresh perspective to the discourse. In particular, I want to explore something of the *experience* of engaging with difference in order to highlight the affective and relational dimensions of inter-religious encounter; I want to challenge and problematize taken-for-granted notions of religious diversity which may underlie philosophical discourse about this topic (where religious diversity is assumed, rather than narrated), and I want to show how feminist and practical theological approaches to the topic might both sharpen and, at places, challenge Professor Margolis' argument. In doing so, I am not offering a standard 'response' but more in the way of a 'riff' (to use a musical analogy) on some of the themes and motifs in Margolis' paper, extemporizing on what I see to be key concerns but taking them up and developing them in my own fashion, in a different key and in a different voice.

## Reflecting on the experience of engaging with the difficult 'other'

I want to start with my experience of engaging with Professor Margolis' paper as a non-philosopher. This experience has been a useful reminder of what it can feel like to be the 'other', the non-native speaker, the non-expert: an experience, I would want to suggest, that is core to the topic of this journal issue; an experience, also, which is quite common in the life of the scholar or researcher, and therefore worthy of consideration in its own right as well as for what light it may shed on the issue of engaging with religious diversity.

I have been preparing these brief comments in Birmingham, England, whilst the UK news has been dominated by images of refugees in their thousands in mainland Europe and by Jeremy Corbyn's early days as new leader of the Labour party (a left-wing member of the Labour party whose election as leader has caused something of a sensation in Britain, upsetting the centrist convergence of the main political parties in recent decades). Both news stories in different ways reflect the challenge to a society to enlarge its thinking and imagination, as well as its borders, in order to accommodate the outsider. It may be fanciful to suppose there is some link between these political issues and the challenge to make sense of a difficult philosophical paper, but I don't think so. As Simone Weil suggested decades ago,[1] the effort to address and resolve an intellectual problem, whatever its nature, can be understood, not merely as an intellectual exercise in its own right but as training for the moral and religious life, if approached with the right attitude.

When we have to work hard to understand another person, a book or an argument, even when we fail, the effort itself changes us. As we stretch our minds and hearts wide enough to allow what is strange and difficult to come close, we may transcend our own limitations and expand our horizons, if only minutely. We may find meaning and value in the other and in our exchange that does not depend on intellectual mastery or even common understanding. In reading a difficult text that eludes my understanding, I may appreciate the quality of the writer's prose, the *way* they form and shape ideas, their craft and inventiveness; just as meeting another person, even – or perhaps especially – when we cannot communicate by words, affords me an opportunity to pay attention to their embodied being, the way they look and sound and inhabit space, the quality of their presence in the world. Such encounters invite me to pay attention to what happens to my own sense of self when I am deprived of linguistic or intellectual proficiency. I want to suggest that such experiences may be useful, even vital, in the endeavour to engage with religious diversity. I speak primarily as a practical theologian, concerned with the affective, spiritual, moral and religious dimensions of this challenge of otherness, yet of course this is also a central philosophical question – the question of how far it is possible to understand the other, across boundaries of language, thought, culture and religious difference; a question I take to be core to the discussion at hand.

## Perspectives from practical and feminist theology

It is no accident that I've started with my experience of reading and responding to Professor Margolis' paper. This is where practical and feminist theologians, as well as poets, tend to start: not with theory, abstraction or argument, but with concrete experience. Practical and feminist theologians are not naïve about the philosophical problems attending the notion of 'experience' (feminist theologians have been deconstructing and problematizing the notion of 'women's experience' for at least 3 decades), yet they suggest that, in rooting scholarly study in lived experience, we may access wisdom not amenable to theoretical analysis alone. Of course, philosophers are interested in ordinary experience just as practical and feminist theologians are interested in theory. But there is a difference in starting point, in methodology and in focus, which may also yield different outcomes.[2] To put it simplistically, practical theologians tend to shape their thinking and theology out of and in the light of practice and lived experience, in inductive fashion, whereas – at least classically – philosophers have worked the other way round, from deductive reason to practice and application. As a pragmatist, Margolis himself has troubled the classical approach of philosophical discourse, although I was surprised that there is not more attention to practice and application in his paper which, at least to me, had a somewhat abstracted air about it. The two approaches may not be entirely antithetical, and each may learn something from the other, yet they tend to represent different conceptions of truth and meaning: personal, relational, narrative, embodied and lived truth as opposed to propositional, rational and conceptual truth. Lived religion pertains much more to the former, whereas formal philosophical as well as theological discourse have tended to occupy the second arena, although much modern theology as well as philosophy has attempted to collapse the watertight boundary (think of Wittgenstein's notion of 'language games' functioning within diverse 'forms of life' and the many theological applications and developments of his approach, from Fergus Kerr to Stanley Hauerwas and Rowan Williams).[3]

Anyhow, to come back to Margolis' paper, I'd like to suggest that both practical and feminist theology might, on the one hand, strengthen, nuance and develop the trajectory which, if I understand him aright, Professor Margolis has offered in his analysis of the nature of religion and, on the other hand, problematize and challenge it in certain regards. In the process, I hope to demonstrate the different approach that practical and feminist theologians might make to the issues of truth, meaning and religious diversity.

Professor Margolis offers a pragmatic account of religious faith which recognizes historical development and change within religious traditions and regards plurality both within and between religions as a 'natural' or inevitable 'given'. Practical and feminist theologies share a similar approach, and offer accounts of religion that might enrich as well as confuse our understanding of religious diversity, problematizing any assumptions we might bring to the debate about where the lines of demarcation lie and how they operate. For, whilst systematic theologians and philosophers are inclined to equate religious faith with the cognitive affirmations enshrined in creeds and confessions, practical and feminist theologians regard such 'espoused theology' as only one among many dimensions of religion. A group of UK practical theologians have recently developed what they call a 'four voices' model of faith[4] that might be useful to this discussion. 'Operant theology' – in other words, how religious believers actually perform and live out their faith – may or may not be in conformity with their 'espoused theology' (what they say they believe), and both of these two modes of faith may or may not conform to the 'normative theology' of their tradition as expressed in its scriptures, creeds and liturgies or the 'formal theology' of trained theologians. One can readily think of individuals or groups who espouse a conservative, perhaps even literalist, reading of the scriptures – say on issues of sexuality, which Margolis singles out as a pertinent contemporary issue – and yet practice a pastoral acceptance and openness to those who live in same-sex relationships that is in tension with their reading of the scriptures. Or, in an opposite direction, there are those who hold to a traditional form of liturgical practice yet espouse non-realist views of God, understanding their practice of worship and prayer in quite different ways from that of a realist believer. And of course, 'operant theology' itself operates at many different levels and in many different ways. Religious believers 'perform' faith through prayer, devotion and public worship as well as through acts of service and social engagement – but also, as Professor Margolis reminds us, through acts of exclusion, violence and warfare. Practical theologians would want to say that such performative acts are not secondary expressions of belief but are, in and of themselves, primary forms of faith. The practice *is* the theology, not merely a secondary expression of it.[5]

Inter-religious encounter, if it is to be more than an academic exercise, needs to pay attention to each of these levels or dimensions of faith, not simply the level of belief. Engagements between adherents of different religious traditions which focus only on the conceptual level (for example, the issue of conflicting truth claims) ignore the multiple dimensions of religious practice and are very likely to overemphasize the significance of belief, on the one hand, and fail to grasp the complex and nuanced ways in which belief needs to be read in relation to the other dimensions or forms of faith, on the other. Even to speak of 'inter-religious dialogue' perhaps gives the game away: the term describes a primarily intellectual exercise of speaking and listening conducted by the (usually male) theologians who are assumed to be the competent spokespersons of their tradition, with a view towards achieving greater understanding of each others' beliefs. This is not a bad aim in itself, but is a limited one which has already decided who and what is important in the exchange, and excludes a great deal of what we might consider to be valuable inter-religious encounter from which philosophy and theology might learn.

For this is not, on the whole, how ordinary believers, including the majority of women, 'do' inter-religious encounter.[6] On the ground, in the streets and schools and businesses of cities like Birmingham and Amsterdam, encounters between people of different faiths and no faith and in-between faith happen every day through personal and professional relationships with colleagues, neighbours and friends, through shared political and social action, and in a rich exchange of spiritual and religious practices. This is named by the Pontifical Council on Interreligious Dialogue as different 'forms of dialogue': the dialogue of life, of action and of religious experience, as well as that of theological exchange,[7] although I would prefer to reserve the term 'dialogue' for theological exchange and speak of the other forms as 'encounter'. This recognition of the broader experience and context of inter-religious encounter is typical of a feminist approach to mission and engagement that Jeannine Hill Fletcher describes as 'fundamentally relational, grounded in friendship and the messiness of actual human lives'.[8] (Her account of three historical case studies of women's inter-religious encounter – in China in the early 1920s and 1930s, in global feminist movements in first-, second- and third-wave feminisms and in Philadelphia in the present – offers fascinating glimpses into the ways in which women have done and still 'do it differently'). If I think of my own experiences of inter-religious encounter, they have been in small, informal networks of women who don't so much want to talk about faith as practice it together and make a difference to each other's lives. I'm thinking of an interfaith group of women who meet monthly in Birmingham to pray together for peace, and who manage to do so without any of the theological difficulties that religious leaders or theologians may raise at the idea of shared prayer across faith boundaries. I'm thinking of the European Women's Synod Movement, which offers an alternative to the official synods of the churches for Christian, Jewish and a few Muslim women across Europe who do not simply want to talk together but to *travel* together (the literal meaning of 'synod') and make decisions that will create better living conditions for women in Europe – and in the current climate, where some European nations are hardening their boundaries in order to prevent movement across borders, such groups may take on a heightened significance, however small and marginal they may appear to be.

Of course, I am not suggesting that the women in these kinds of groups or networks all think or act in the same way or take a common stance in regard to religious and political issues. Far from it. Notions of intersectionality and hybridity which have become common parlance in post-colonial and queer as well as feminist discourse, disallow and dismantle optimistic mythologies of 'sisterhood' and compel feminists to pay close attention to their own participation in axes of power. Moving away from unitary notions of the self, essentialized understandings of race, gender or sexuality and homogenous notions of religion, these discourses invite us to recognize the fluidity and hybridity of our complex allegiances and shifting identities. Nevertheless, and whilst eschewing essentialized understandings of gender, in my experience, the lines of demarcation between women are not always where men might expect them to be, and the kinds of issues which dominate discussion amongst academic philosophers and theologians or religious leaders are frequently not key concerns for women or for ordinary believers, whose agendas are different. In feminist groups, for example, religious and denominational differences between women are often not as significant as the economic, cultural and ethnic differences that divide women from each other and from access to resources. At the same time, feminists may be more likely to join forces across religious divides that might seem more significant to others in order to challenge and critique patriarchal religion. Rather than consider theological differences between Jewish, Christian and Muslim understandings of God, for example, they might be more likely to consider how patriarchal models of God in each tradition have functioned to legitimize male power, not only over women and children but also over other species and the earth itself. Perhaps precisely because women have tended to occupy a more marginal status in religious traditions, at least until recently, they may be more willing, through their experience of marginalization, to critique and transform the faith they have received. Whilst feminists would agree with Margolis that religion needs to 'adjust' to support species survival, many would want to offer a sharper and more trenchant critique of the ways in which religious discourse and practice have been antithetical to the flourishing of other species and the earth itself. Patriarchal models of God as well as notions of 'man' as God's vice-regent on earth have been sharply critiqued by ecofeminist theologians and philosophers, along with models of rationality and spirituality that privilege discursive reason over the body, the passions and relationality.[9] Perhaps Margolis does not go far enough in his recognition of the philosophical, as well as the religious, roots of violent and world-destroying forms of religion; nor does he appear aware of the work of ecofeminists who address precisely this issue.

## Conclusion

To conclude these brief remarks and attempt a summary of my gist: difference isn't always where we expect it to be, and what we see to be key differences will depend to a large extent on our context, social location and political agenda. And of course, our perceptions as well as our experiences of difference will also keep shifting. What we take to be significant boundaries or dilemmas will look very different from elsewhere and will not map directly onto others' experience or perceptions.

Far from such a recognition being a cause for despair, it should be a reason for intellectual as well as spiritual curiosity and commitment. In a fascinating paper, Hill Fletcher proposes that, paradoxically, it is possible to 'enact solidarity through hybrid identities' much more effectively than through undifferentiated, unitary selves.[10] As we recognize how complex and hybrid our *own* shifting identities are, so we may be less inclined to project onto others naïve and simplistic assumptions about *their* identity and, at the same time, we may be more likely to find points of connection across multiple difference. Knowing how complex and multifaceted my own identity and allegiances are, I will not expect the 'other' to be any less complex, and I will not assume from the outset that I can predict what they believe, how they will behave and how they interpret the diverse traditions from which they draw. This makes each and every encounter across difference – whatever the difference we are talking about – so much more fascinating, complex and unpredictable than any model of pluralism is able to account for. Practical theologians, with their attention to lived experience and their models of how lived religion actually functions across and between multiple dimensions, may have something particularly valuable to offer the philosophers here, situating discourse about truth and meaning within a wider frame of reference.

Which brings me back to where I started: the intellectual and moral effort required to engage with difference, and the way in which the effort itself, even if it never entirely succeeds, changes and expands us in the process.

## Acknowledgements

I am grateful to Professor Dirk-Martin Grübe for the invitation to respond to a paper that is well outside my field and my comfort zone and to Professor Margolis for a text that has stretched and challenged my understanding.

## Notes

1  Weil, *Waiting on God*, 32–37.
2  For a more systematic development of a practical theological approach to interfaith engagement, see Gaston, "Towards a Practical Theology."
3  For example, Williams, "The suspicion of suspicion"; Kerr, *Theology after Wittgenstein*, and Hauerwas, *Character and the Christian Life*.
4  Cameron et al., *Talking About God in Practice*, 13.
5  See Graham, *Transforming Practice*, for a British exemplar of such an approach to practice.
6  I deliberately speak of 'inter-religious encounter' in favour of 'dialogue' in order to draw attention to the broader range of activities that ordinary believers engage in, when relating to members of other faiths, that go beyond debate and discussion, and to situate such dialogue within a social and relational context.
7  Pontifical Council on Interreligious Dialogue, "Dialogue and Proclamation," section 3.42.
8  Fletcher, *Motherhood as Metaphor*, xii.
9  The work of feminist philosophers of religion such as Grace Jantzen comes to mind here; her life project, developed in several volumes, was to critique forms of Christian theology and practice that valorized death, violence and dualistic views of human as well as planetary life, and to develop a theology rooted in natality.
10 Fletcher, "Shifting identity," 20.

## Bibliography

Cameron, H., D. Bhatt, C. Duce, J. Sweeney, and C. Watkins. *Talking About God in Practice: Theological Action Research and Practical Theology.* London: SCM, 2010.

Fletcher, J. H. "Shifting Identity: The Contribution of Feminist Thought to Theologies of Religious Pluralism." *Journal of Feminist Studies in Religion* 19, no. 2 (2003): 5–24.

Fletcher, J. H. *Motherhood as Metaphor: Engendered Interreligious Dialogue.* Bronx, NY: Fordham University Press, 2013.

Gaston, R. "Towards a Practical Theology of Inter Faith Engagement." In *Twenty-First Century Theologies of Religions: Retrospection and New Frontiers*, edited by E. Harris, P. Hedges, and S. Hettiarachchi. Leiden: E.J. Brill, 2015.

Graham, E. *Transforming Practice: Pastoral Theology in an Age of Uncertainty.* London: Mowbray, 1996.

Hauerwas, S. *Character and the Christian Life.* San Antonio, TX: San Antonio University Press, 1985.

Jantzen, G. *Becoming Divine: Towards a Feminist Philosophy of Religion.* Manchester: University of Manchester, 1998.

Jantzen, G. *Foundations of Violence 1: Death and the Displacement of Beauty.* London: Routledge, 2004.

Jantzen, G. *Violence to Eternity: Death and the Displacement of Beauty.* London: Routledge, 2008.

Jantzen, G. *A Place of Springs: Death and the Displacement of Beauty.* London: Routledge, 2009.

Kerr, F. *Theology after Wittgenstein.* London: SPCK, 1997.

Margolis, J. "Uncertain Musings about the State of the World and Religion's Contribution." *International Journal of Philosophy and Theology* 75, no. 5 (2015): 397–406.

Pontifical Council on Interreligious Dialogue. "Dialogue and Proclamation: Reflection and orientations on interreligious dialogue and the proclamation of the gospel of Jesus Christ", Rome. Accessed May 19, 1991. http://www.vatican.va/roman_curia/pontifical_councils/interelg/docu ments/rc_pc_interelg_doc_19051991_dialogue-and-proclamatio_en.html (section 3.42)

Weil, S. "Reflections on the Right Use of School Studies with a View to the Love of God." In *Waiting on God*, 32–37. Abingdon: Routledge, 2010.

Williams, R. "The Suspicion of Suspicion: Wittgenstein and Bonhoeffer." In *Wrestling with Angels: Conversations in Modern Theology*, edited by M. Higton, 186–202. London: SCM, 2007.

# Justified religious difference: a constructive approach to religious diversity

Dirk-Martin Grube

In this paper, I provide a novel approach to the issue of religious diversity: I reject classical pluralist approaches to the issue, such as John Hick's, and argue that their attempts to construe commonalities between the religions are contrived. The reason that they attempt to find commonalities at all costs is that they presuppose a bivalent notion of truth according to which that which is different is false. I suggest that, in order to get a robust theory on religious diversity off the ground, we should rely on the notion of justification rather than that of bivalent truth. Justification is pluralizable, dependent upon the (epistemic) circumstances, whereas bivalent truth is not. Armed with a pluralizable notion of justification, we can acknowledge that other religious beliefs are genuinely different without necessarily being false: They can be justified, given the (epistemic) circumstances a believer of a different religion is in. Perceiving religious differences in this way allows to liberate the interreligious dialogue from the pressure to find commonalities between religions at all costs, to respect the religious Other in her Otherness, and to 'mirror' one's own religion in light of other religions.

In the Netherlands and other countries, Jews, Christians, Muslims, Hindus, Buddhists, and adherents of other religions live side by side. Those different religions prescribe different ways of life for their adherents and claim different things to be true. Think for instance of differences between concepts of heaven or paradise as in the three Abrahamic religions and that of a union with the One or Nondual as in some Indian religions.

Given those differences, we need a theoretical framework within which they can be dealt with in a constructive fashion. By 'constructive fashion', I mean a fashion which allows for tolerance and respect for religions other than the home religion.

In the following, I will sketch such a framework. I call it 'justified religious difference'. My claim is that it allows for tolerance and respect and, equally important to me, is philosophically viable: It is based upon one of the most promising viewpoints in current epistemology, epistemology being the theory of knowledge.

Before delving into that, however, let me sketch where I come from: Theologically, I hold a Christian viewpoint, philosophically, a pragmatist one in the broad sense of the term. Most of my work is at the intersection between philosophy and religion. Opposed to much common wisdom, I think that there are good *theological* reasons for respecting other religions. Yet, I will not delve into theology today but will focus solely on philosophy, in line with this conference's overall topic.

My exposure to religions other than the Christian, one has predominantly been by way of personal encounters: Many of my friends were and are Muslims and Jews. Although my following contribution will be mostly of a theoretical sort, I think that its roots lie in those personal encounters. I consider it to be the theoretical wrap-up of what happens when believers of different religious traditions encounter each other respectfully and dialogue in an honest fashion.

I will proceed in 10 sections: in Section 1, I discuss one of the best-known approaches to religious tolerance, viz. pluralism, in Section 2–6, I cover the theoretical background upon which 'justified religious difference' rests, in Sections 7–10, I bring the theoretical discussion to bear upon the issue of the interreligious dialogue.

## 1. Religious pluralism

In the following, I mean by 'classical pluralist paradigm' or, simply, 'pluralism' the approaches in religion which have emerged since the 1960s, such as John Hick's and Paul Knitter's. Although they come from a particular, viz. Christian background, their guiding intention is to respect non-Christian religions as well.

*The* basic tool with which they attempt to achieve their guiding intention is to minimize or neutralize the differences between the divergent religions. To that end, they postulate some kind of unity between the different religions.[1] This postulated unity is located either *within* the empirical religions or *beyond* them.

An example of the former are Knitter's later works, in which he emphasizes the concept of 'eco-human justice' as the common core of religion, that is, a concept of well-being for humanity, in particular, for the poor, and for our fragile planet.[2]

An example of the latter, that is, of postulating a unity *beyond* the empirical religions, is Hick's concept of a transcendent *'Real an sich'*. Hick postulates it to lie behind the current empirical world religions. Those religions relate to the *'Real an sich'* in the same way, in which empirical reality relates to Immanuel Kant's *'Ding an sich'*: They are adumbrations, in Dutch: *'afschaduwingen'* of the *'Real an sich'*. But they are not identical with it since it is unfathomable. Being unfathomable, the empirical religions cannot claim to capture it. Given this difference between the *'Real an sich'* and the empirical religions, they should moderate their claims to absolute religious truth. This moderation is the basis for tolerating other religions.[3]

Although I appreciate the pluralists' attempts to respect other religions, I doubt their success. Attempts to find a unity within or beyond the empirical religions fail in my view. Searching for a common core á la Knitter is a tour de force: Although I have personally some sympathy with his concept of 'eco-human justice', intellectual honesty demands to admit that by far not all religions share it.[4]

And attempts to find some unity *beyond* the empirical religions are highly problematic on theoretical grounds. Hick's famous postulate of a *'Real an sich'* has thus been criticized heavily. The reason is that, if the *'Real an sich'* is truly unfathomable, nothing meaningful can be said about its relation to the empirical religions – certainly not that the current ones relate to it and previous religions did not, as Hick suggests. Hick magnifies the problems which inhere already in Kant's *'Ding an sich'* by transferring it into the theorizing on religious diversity.[5]

Generalizing from those examples, I suggest that pluralism fails. We should thus look for an alternative to it. In order to develop such an alternative, I will look in the following into a presupposition which many pluralists and other people discussing religious diversity share, viz. *bivalence*. The critique of bivalence will serve then as a springboard for developing the alternative I suggest.

## 2. Bivalence and the interreligious dialogue

Let me begin by explaining the term: Bivalence is a logical principle which implies that statements have exactly one and not more than one truth value. They are *either* true *or* false. A logic satisfying this principle is called a two-value or bivalent logic. For today's purposes, I subsume the negative formulation of bivalence, the law of excluded middle, under 'bivalence'.[6]

Bivalence understood in this sense implies a particular way of dealing with that which is genuinely different: It implies that, if position A is true and position B differs from A, B *must* be false. Please note that B's falsity is not affirmed after careful scrutiny but by default, viz. simply by virtue of the fact that *A* is held to be true. Under bivalent parameters, there is no other choice than to consider B to be false. Since only A *or* B can be true but not both, B must be false if A is true. I summarize this point by suggesting that bivalence implies an *equation between difference and falsity*.

I suspect that many pluralist and related attempts presuppose this equation. It is the backdrop against which their attempts to minimize or neutralize the differences between the religions are to be understood. They are driven by the anxious desire to downplay difference, since difference is taken to equal falsity. Since they wish to avoid considering other religions to be false, they *must* demonstrate that they are not that different. Under the auspices of this equation, they have no other choice. The equation between difference and falsity thus breeds the pressure to minimize difference.

Yet, pressures of this sort jeopardize honest communication. An interreligious dialogue being pursued under this pressure is thus suspicious of overemphasizing similarities between the religions at the cost of their dissimilarities.

And a dialogue pursued under this pressure is in jeopardy of losing sight of the religious Other *in her Otherness*: If I overemphasize the Other's similarities with myself, I am in danger of making a caricature of her rather than to grasp her authentic being.

Since this is the result of pursuing the interreligious dialogue under the equation between difference and falsity, we should question this equation and the principle of bivalence upon which it rests.

## 3. Margolis' criticism of bivalence

One of the most prominent critics of bivalence is Joseph Margolis who rejects bivalence understood as a general logical principle, supposed to hold in all domains of inquiry. He argues that there are certain domains in which this principle does *not* apply. The prime example of such a domain is the world of culture, for instance literary and art criticism, the interpretation of history, moral, legal, and prudential matters. In this domain, the objects are of such a sort that they cannot be judged to be true or false in a clear-cut fashion.[7]

Margolis suggests to substitute a two-valued logic with a many-valued logic which relies on values such as 'indeterminate': We are at times incapable of deciding effectively whether objects pertaining to the world of culture are true or false but have to leave this question open. There is thus more than only the bivalent pair of truth values, 'true' and 'false'. There is a third one, 'indeterminate', and there are probably more.[8]

I agree with Margolis's critique of bivalence. Yet, as far as the lessons to be learnt from this critique, I will explore a somewhat different route today: Rather than suggesting to retreat to a many-valued logic, I suggest to go beyond the realm of logic and truth altogether. My suggestion is to employ the notion of *justification* rather than that of truth in cases in which bivalence does not apply.

## 4. The notion of justification

The term justification can be used in a variety of contexts. For example, the Protestant theologian can propose that the sinner is justified in God's eyes. Yet, I do not have such a theological use in mind but an *epistemological* one. An example of this use is to say that an agent is justified in holding a belief because she has acquired it in epistemologically praiseworthy ways.

Let me spell out what I mean by the epistemological sense of justification in three short points:

-First, justification differs from truth: the latter is attributed to beliefs, whereas justification is attributed to *agents holding beliefs*. An agent can hold a belief on justified or unjustified grounds. The question whether she is justified in holding a belief depends on a number of factors, for instance whether she has carefully mustered the available evidence.

-Second, justification kicks in only where truth is uncertain. Now, I believe that there are many areas in which truth questions are undecidable, ranging from the world of culture, via quantum mechanics and complex geological and medical issues to religion. Yet, there are issues where the truth -question can be decided. In those cases, the question of justification does not arise. For example, if a person asserts that the traffic light is green whereas it is red, I do not ask myself whether she is justified to do so but whether she is color-blind. The same goes for the example of the racist, with the help of which Prof. Wolterstorff challenged my account of justification in his contribution: If the racist bases his beliefs upon obviously false assumptions, say, on the mistaken assumption that a particular race is genetically superior to another race, the question whether he is justified to hold his beliefs does not arise. Even if he was subjectively justified – say, because he is one-sidedly indoctrinated and too dumb to realize it – this would be epistemologically irrelevant – although it may be relevant in other respects, say, juridical ones. My point is that in cases in which the truth question can be decided, truth takes precedence over justification.

-Third, quite like truth, justification is a *normative* concept. Saying that an agent is justified in holding a belief is to pass a value judgement on her epistemological behavior. Justification can thus *not* be reduced to some kind of sociological or other descriptive theory since this would deprive it of its normative dimension.

Thus, my suggestion to substitute truth differs from some postmodernist suggestions to substitute it. I think for instance of Richard Rorty's suggestion that 'Truth is what your peers will let you get away with'.[9] This is a characteristic example of a sociological reduction which deprives the concept of truth of its normative function.

Yet, this normative function is indispensable for what we want an account of truth or its substitute to deliver: We want it to enable us to distinguish epistemologically praise-worthy from epistemologically blameworthy behavior. I think that, if specified along the lines suggested above, justification is capable of enabling us to distinguish between both sorts of behavior.

## 5. The plurality of justification

Since the beginning of this century, justification is heavily discussed in epistemology.[10] This discussion has brought to light that justification differs from truth: it is more strongly context-dependent than truth is. For example, epistemologists like Jonathan Kvanvig suggest that what a person is justified to believe depends on her perspective, say, on what information is available to her at a given moment.[11] Thus, whether a person is justified to hold a belief depends to a good extent on the epistemological context, that is, the epistemological circumstances, she happens to be in.

Yet, it would be odd to suggest that the *truth* of this belief depends on the epistemological circumstances a particular individual is in. Suggesting this would make truth as contingent as those circumstances are – which flatly contradicts all we know about truth.[12]

Thus, justification is plural in way in which truth isn't: There are different perspectives, different epistemological contexts which allow to justify different but equally legitimate beliefs.

Let me explain, what I mean with the help of an example taken from the realm of history: Say, person A explains the aggressive attitude Germany took right before the First World War in purely materialistic terms. Maybe she suggests that it wished to expand its overseas colonies. Person B, however, may explain this attitude in non-materialistic terms, say, by suggesting that Germans and particularly their emperor suffered from minority complexes since Germany was not recognized as a peer among the then leading nations in Europe.

My point is that both materialistic *and* non-materialistic explanations can be justified, although the beliefs implied in them differ. Thus, persons A and B can *both* be justified to hold different beliefs on the same issue. Thus, a plurality of different beliefs can be legitimate.

## 6. Acknowledging genuine otherness versus claiming intellectual Monopolies á la Dawkins

Let me conclude this theoretical part with a general reflection.

I think that there are two fundamentally different attitudes toward life: The first is to acknowledge that other people hold beliefs which differ from mine but are nevertheless justified or legitimate. This is the attitude which acknowledges genuine Otherness. Obviously, I favor this attitude.

Opposed to, it is the attitude which postulates an intellectual *monopoly* for a particular viewpoint. This attitude has a long history, defended for instance by parts of the Christian Church. Most recently, however, it is defended not so much by theists but by *atheists*, the prime example being Richard *Dawkins'*. Characteristic for monopolists of this sort is the use of a twofold strategy: First, they claim principled cognitive privileges for their own group. For example, naturalists like Dawkins call themselves 'the brights'.[13] Second, they explain the cognitive inferiority of competing views in paternalistic ways. I come back to that below.

For now, however, I would like to remind you that what attitude you hold is not only some idle game but has serious intellectual, cultural, and political consequences. Those of us who acknowledge genuine Otherness will respect persons who hold viewpoints which differ from ours rather than regard them to be cognitively inferior. They work toward creating open-minded intellectual environments, which can deal constructively with different viewpoints, including different religious and related viewpoints. For example, they favor a discourse culture which makes the dialogue between those different viewpoints fruitful rather than one which monopolizes one particular viewpoint at the cost of all alternative ones.

I suggest that those of us who respect genuine Otherness should be prepared to defend the intellectual, cultural, and political settings which allow for it against their current threats. We are proud to have cast out theistic monopolies and do not wish monopolism to sneak back in through the atheist backdoor.


## 7. 'Justified religious difference'

Although challenging atheists is a hobby of mine, I will return to the issue of religious diversity now and bring the theoretical discussion to bear upon this issue: My suggestions to abstain from bivalence and to pluralize justification provide the basis for the framework I recommend for dealing with this issue, that is, for *'justified religious difference'*.

The core of 'justified religious difference' consists of applying the insight that difference can be justified to religion. In a nutshell: Since different people can be justified in holding different beliefs – given their different perspectives and different epistemological contexts – different *religious* people can be justified in holding different *religious* beliefs – given their different perspectives and different epistemological contexts. As little as, we have to condemn all deviant beliefs to be false – if we acknowledge justified difference, we do not have to condemn all deviant *religious* beliefs to be false – if we acknowledge justified difference in religion.

The upshot of 'justified religious difference' is thus that you can be justified in holding your Jewish, Islamic, Buddhist, Hinduist, etc. beliefs, given *your* epistemic circumstances, while I can be simultaneously justified in holding my Christian beliefs, given *my* epistemic circumstances.[14]

Now, what does the interreligious dialogue look like under the auspices of 'justified religious difference'? I will answer that question in the remaining three sections.


## 8. 'Justified religious difference' and the function of the interreligious dialogue

Let me remind you of the strong pressures under which the interreligious dialogue is pursued under the auspices of bivalence. I mean the pressure to downplay differences between the religions because difference equals falsity under bivalent parameters. People wishing to avoid having to consider other religions to be false are thus under pressure to emphasize the similarities between the religions at the cost of their dissimilarities. This pressure jeopardizes an honest and open-ended interreligious dialogue.

Under the auspices of 'justified religious difference', however, the interreligious dialogue is liberated from such pressures. Its results are open. If we find similarities between our religions, let's celebrate that. When talking to my Muslim and Jewish friends, I am often very happy to discover similarities – say, in the area of what I consider to be valuable resources to resist the ruthlessness and superficiality our Western culture as well as others have maneuvered themselves into.

Yet, I agree with Prof. Wolterstorff's insistence that finding common ground is not the sole goal of the interreligious dialogue. Let's not be disappointed if we do *not* find similarities between our religions. Above all, let's resist the temptation to reinterpret differences as similarities with the help of this or that hermeneutical trick. Tolerance and respect for deviating religions do *not* depend on their similarities to the home religion. Rather, they depend on the knowledge that the religious Other can be justified to hold her deviant religious beliefs coupled with the assurance that this knowledge does not jeopardize the legitimacy of the home religion.

An open dialogue does not prematurely foreclose the possibility that all religions relate to one and the same transcendent reality. I do not wish to be taken to foreclose this possibility. But the difference with Hick is that I leave this question open to investigation rather than to make my account of religious diversity contingent upon a positive answer to it. I suggest that we are better off devoting our energies to deal with religious differences in a constructive fashion, say, provide the proper discourse environments for them, rather than trying desperately to find commonalities between religions.

In sum, 'justified religious difference' provides the opportunity to pursue the interreligious dialogue in an open spirit. It stays away from exerting pressure on its outcome. I thus hope that it helps to pursue this dialogue in as honest a fashion as possible.

## 9. 'Justified religious difference' and respecting the other in her otherness

An important consequence of the knowledge that the Other is justified in holding the religious beliefs she holds is respect for her religious Otherness. This is the point which is so strongly emphasized in the French-speaking philosophico-religious tradition, say, when insisting on the notion of 'absolute hospitability'.[15] I agree with this point – although I would like to add that I part company with French thinkers such as Jacques Derrida where they succumb to philosophical relativism and hold politically irresponsible views which ignore the *limits* of tolerating Otherness.

Yet, today, my point is not to sketch the limits of tolerance but to make a case for the view that religious differences can be justified and draw out the consequences of this view. One such consequence is to respect the Other *in her Otherness*. 'In her Otherness' is important in so far as it marks the difference with intellectual monopolism: Respecting her this way implies to stay away from postulating principled cognitive privileges and from providing paternalistic explanations for the Other's Otherness.

By 'paternalistic explanations' I mean 'explanations' of the Other's Otherness which imply a principled imbalance in cognitive status. An example is the suggestion that you are not as bright as I am and *that* that is the reason why you hold the beliefs you hold – whereas, if you were as bright as I am, you would not hold the beliefs you hold.

The effect of using paternalistic explanations is that the challenge of the Other's Otherness is neutralized: They provide a legitimation for ignoring it. After all, the Other's viewpoint is inferior to mine. Since I occupy the high grounds, I can afford to ignore her inferior viewpoint.

Few paternalistic explanations are as crude as this one is. Yet, substitute 'bright' with 'Enlightened' and you get much of the religious history of the West into picture. Religious history indebted to the Enlightenment is full of paternalistic explanations which 'explain' the Otherness of other religions by their inferiority.

A justified religious difference approach excludes all kinds of paternalistic explanations, since it excludes principled privileges: Once I have realized that you are *justified* in believing the religious beliefs you hold, there is no need to explain them. Rather than explaining them, I can *accept* them as being different or can go even one step further and regard them to be potential challenges to my view.

Obviously, only *paternalistic* explanations are excluded under the auspices of 'justified religious difference'. Yet, explanations of Otherness which respect the Other as a peer are still very welcome.

## 10. 'Justified religious difference' and the function of arguments

Given 'justified religious difference', should we stop providing arguments for the religious beliefs we hold? Not at all. After all, the beliefs we hold are *our* beliefs and, being reflective persons, we should be capable of providing arguments for them. Yet, we should be acutely aware of what *function* those arguments have. Let me clarify this function with the help of an example.

Being a Lutheran Christian living in the Netherlands, I find myself sometimes involved in discussions with Calvinists. In those discussions, I usually provide arguments what Lutheranism consists of and why I endorse it and my discussion partner does the same for Calvinism. The point of those discussions is to come to a better understanding of each other's religions. An important side effect is to learn more about one's own religious beliefs by 'mirroring' them in light of other religious beliefs.

But the point is *not* to convert each other. At the end of the discussion, I do not expect my discussion partner to convert to Lutheranism but rather respect her in her Calvinist Otherness – hoping that she respects me in my Lutheran Otherness.

Under the auspices of 'justified religious difference', the provision of arguments in the context of the interreligious dialogue is to be reconstructed along similar lines: Its primary function is to 'mirror' one's own beliefs and to understand other people's beliefs but not to convert them.

Much has been said, yet, much more has been left unsaid. I am painfully aware that today's emphasis upon the legitimacy of religious differences has the effect that talk about religious differences which are *il*legitimate has been neglected. Let me thus just say in passing that I consider the framework of 'justified religious difference' to be particularly well equipped to deal with *il*legitimate beliefs – the flip side of talking about religious differences being justified is obviously that some religious differences are *un*justified. In order to discriminate at this point, criteria allowing to distinguish between justified and unjustified beliefs need to be developed. I could not do this today but hope to take up this and related issues in the future.[16]

### Notes

1. See, for example, Heleen Maat's thesis that pluralists postulate a 'uniformity in diversity' (*Religious Diversity*, 47).
2. See Knitter, *One Earth Many Religions*, 122.
3. See Hick, *An Interpretation of Religion*, 233.
4. See also the critique in Maat, *Religious Diversity*, 52.
5. See, for example, the more thorough critique in Grube, 'Die irreduzible Vielfalt der Religionen', 45.
6. For the notion of bivalence, see, for example, Béziau, 'Bivalence, excluded middle', 73, and, for a more general background, the introduction by Goble, *The Blackwell Guide*, 1; for the notion of excluded middle or *tertium non datur*, see, for example, Dummett, *Truth and Other Enigmas*, xxviii.
7. See Margolis, *The Truth about Relativism*, 18.
8. Ibid., 20 et al.
9. In *Philosophy and the Mirror of Nature*, 176, Rorty describes attempts 'to make truth something more than what Dewey called '*warranted assertibility*'. In describing this 'something more', he explains it with 'more than what our peers will, *ceteris paribus*, let us get away with saying'. Although Rorty does not propose this characterization of truth explicitly here, it is commonly associated with his name.
10. I think of publications such as BonJour and Sosa, *Epistemic Justification*, 35 and 219.
11. See Kvanvig, Propositionalism and the Perspectival, 9.

12. Even Rorty acknowledges the existence of a difference between truth and justification (see Rorty, *Truth and Progress*, 2); see also Stout's reconstruction of this difference in Stout, *Democracy and Tradition*, 231.
13. See, for example, http://www.the-brights.net/.
14. This result resembles closely the upshot of Gotthold Ephraim Lessing's famous ring-parable in 'Nathan the Wise': Lessing argues that the truth of the Jewish, Christian, and Islamic religious beliefs is indeterminate. Given this indeterminacy, justification kicks in. Yet, justification is intrinsically plural. Thus, adherents of all three religions are justified to hold their religious beliefs – an argument that can easily be extended to other religious beliefs as well (for a more detailed reconstruction of Lessing's argument, see Grube, 'Justification rather than Truth', 357–359.
15. Derrida, *Acts of Religion*, 230.
16. This article is a (slightly) revised version of the inaugural lecture I held on 24 September 2015 at the Vrije Universiteit, Amsterdam and is modified in comparison to the published version of this lecture with the Free University Press (Amsterdam).

## Bibliography

Béziau, J.-Y. "Bivalence, Excluded Middle and Non Contradiction." In *The Logica Yearbook 2003*, edited by L. Behounek, 73–84. Prague: Academy of Sciences, 2003.

BonJour, L., and E. Sosa, et al. *Epistemic Justification. Internalism vs. Externalism, Foundations vs. Virtues*. Malden, Oxford: Blackwell, 2003.

Derrida, J. *Acts of Religion*. (ed. and with an introduction by Gil Anidjar). New York, NY: Routlege, 2002.

Dummett, M. *Truth and Other Enigmas*. Cambridge: Harvard University Press, 1978.

Goble, L. ed. *The Blackwell Guide to Philosophical Logic*. New York, NY: Wiley-Blackwell, 2002.

Grube, D.-M. "Justification rather than Truth: Gotthold Ephraim Lessing's Defence of Positive Religion in the Ring-Parable." *Bijdragen International Journal in Philosophy and Theology* 66, no. 1 (2005): 357–378.

Grube, D.-M. "Die Irreduzible Vielfalt Der Religionen Und Die Einheit Der Wahrheit." In *Wahrheitsanprüche Der Weltreligionen. Konturen Gegenwärtiger Religionsphilosophie*, edited by F. H. Christian Danz, 41–66. Neukirchen: Neukirchener Verlag, 2006.

Hick, J. *An Interpretation of Religion. Human Responses to the Transcendent*. (first edition 1989). Basingstoke: Palgrave/MacMillan, 2004.

Knitter, P. F. *One Earth Many Religions. Multifaith Dialogue and Global Responsibility*. Maryknoll, NY: Orbis, 1995.

Kvanvig, J. "Propositionalism and the Perspectival Character of Justification." *American Philosophical Quarterly* 40, no. 1 (2003): 3–17.

Maat, H. "Religious Diversity, Intelligibility and Truth." dissertation. Boekencentrum Academic, 2009.

Margolis, J. *The Truth about Relativism*. Cambridge, Oxford: Blackwell, 1991.

Rorty, R. *Philosophy and the Mirror of Nature*. Princeton: Princeton University Press, 1979.

Rorty, R. *Truth and Progress. Philosophical Papers*. Vol. 3. Cambridge: Cambridge University Press, 1998.

Sosa, E., and E. Villanueva, eds. *Epistemology*, Philosophical Issues 14. Boston: Blackwell, 2004.

Stout, J. *Democracy and Tradition*. Princeton: Princeton University Press, 2004.

Wolterstorff, N. Obligation, Entitlement, and Rationality, in: *Contemporary Debates in Epistemology*, edited by Matthias Steup, Ernest Sosa, 326–338, 342–343Malden: Blackwell, 2005.

# An epistemic argument for tolerance

René van Woudenberg

In this paper I first take a critical look at Grube's allegiance to the idea that bivalence should be rejected as it can serve the cause of religious toleration. I argue that bivalence is not what Grube says it is, and that rejection of bivalence comes at a very high price that we should not be willing to pay. Next I analyze Grube's argument for religious toleration – an argument that does not involve the rejection of bivalence. I argue that the argument is unconvincing because there exists no relation between epistemic justification and toleration. (I also note problems with the notion of 'justi-fication' as used by Grube.)

Many years ago the beat poet Steve Turner wrote the poem 'Modern Thinker's Creed'. One of its stanzas says:

> We believe
> all religions
> are basically the same.
> At least
> The one that we read was.
> They all believe in love and goodness.
> They only differ in matters of
> creation, sin, heaven, hell, God and salvation.[1]

I think Dirk-Martin Grube, to whose paper this is a response,[2] should like this stanza, as it expresses, in an ironical fashion, the 'pluralist' view of the relationship between the world's religions that he opposes. At the same time, it hints at some problems of the view that Grube also mentions. Let me explain.

The core of the pluralist view is that the world's religions are, somehow, 'one', and that whatever differences exist between the religions, are inessential and hence unim-portant. On this view, religious differences should not be focused on in the inter religious dialogue. The one-ness or unity of the world's religions, on the pluralist view, is the basis for religious toleration. In Hick's pluralist view, for example, the world's religions are all geared toward 'the Real an sich', but as 'the Real an sich' is unfathomable, none of the world's religions, or rather their adherents, can or should lay claim to absolute truth. They should moderate their claims. And this moderation is presented as the basis for religious toleration.

Grube has problems with the pluralist view, but not with the pluralist's call for religious toleration.[3] Rather, his problem is with the pluralist's *argument* for that call.

He therefore aims to provide an alternative argument for toleration. In this short reply to Grube's paper, I will proceed as follows. I first recount what I take to be Grube's key problem with the pluralist view: its commitment to the logical principle of bivalence. I shall argue that the rejection of bivalence is deeply problematic – especially in the context in which he wants to put that rejection to work. Next I will examine Grube's own argument for religious toleration, and point to some problematic features.

## Bivalence as presupposition of pluralism

Pluralism is problematic, Grube rightly says, because it 'breeds the pressure to minimize difference' (421). And he wants to reject it not just on the ground that it breeds this attitude, but because there is something inherently problematic in pluralism. And what he thinks is inherently problematic in pluralism is that pluralism presupposes bivalence. In the wake of his Doktorvater Joseph Margolis, he then goes on to reject bivalence. (Now I should think that giving up bivalence is a council of despair; it is the very last thing one should do. If one wants, like me,[4] to reject pluralism one should first explore other ways. The reason for this is that our common practices of argument, deduction, and reasoning all rely on the validity of this principle. We do not really know what it would be like to think, to argue, or to do science without relying on bivalence.)

The logical principle of bivalence, Grube says, entails that declarative statements 'have exactly one and not more than one truth value' (421). Bivalence, he says, is the thought that declarative statements are either true or false.[5] As a characterization of bivalence, however, this is not exactly right. For first there are declarative statements that have no truth value. Think of such statements as 'When I stood up from my chair, my lap vanished', or ' Her dream weighed 50 kilo'. These statements have no truth value because they *make no sense*. But this does not contradict bivalence. In order for a statement to have a truth value, it must at the very least make sense. There are other kinds of statements that have no truth value, for example the statement 'John sat to the right of Nico'.[6] This statement has no truth value because it is *incomplete*: it does not contain the crucial information from whose point of view John sat to the right of Nico. But this does not contradict bivalence. For a statement to have truth value, it must be complete. Furthermore, some statements are both true and false. Think of such statements as 'Hilary Clinton is still running'. This statement is true – Hilary Clinton is still running for presidency. At the same time this statement is false – she is not (let us suppose) exercising, but sound asleep. This statement is both true and false, because it is *ambiguous*. But this does not contradict bivalence. For a statement to have one truth value, it must be unambiguous. A better phrasing of bivalence, then, is this: every declarative statement that is meaningful, complete and unambiguous is either true or false.[7] I take it that Grube agrees with this.

Grube says that bivalence 'implies that, if proposition A is true and proposition B differs from A, B *must* be false' (421). But this is not the case: bivalence does not imply this. Take, for example, for A: 'Bayern München won' and for B: 'A German team won'. These propositions clearly differ from each other. Yet it is not the case that if A is true, B *must* be false. As a matter of fact, in this case, if A is true, then B must be true too! Or to take another example, suppose A is 'Goethe wrote *Die Leiden des junges Werthers*' and B is 'Werner Bergengruen wrote *Der spanische Rosenstock*'. Then A and B are clearly different. Yet it is not the case that if A is true, B must be false. As a matter of fact, both propositions are true. And no one who adopts bivalence thinks otherwise: no one thinks that bivalence implies that if propositions A and B are different, then if A is true, B must be false. What bivalence *does* imply is that *if A entails not-B*, then if A is true, B must be false. I take it that Grube agrees with this as well.

But then he will also have to agree that his statement that 'bivalence implies an *equation between difference and falsity*' (421) is misleading, and as stated simply false. What *is* correct is the following modified statement: 'bivalence implies that if proposition A entails proposition not-B, then if A is true, B must be false'.

Since Grube thinks his original statement is true, I assume that he will think my improved, modified statement is certainly true: bivalence has the implication stated. But since he rejects the implication (viz. that, with my added qualification, difference = falsity), he boldly reject bivalence, at least *in the domain of religious discourse*.

But what does it mean to reject bivalence? It must mean, given Grube's own formulation of bivalence, that it is not the case that if proposition A is true and proposition B differs from A, B *must* be false. And if we take the improved formulation of bivalence that I offered, it must mean this: it is not the case that if proposition A entails proposition not-B, then if A is true, B must be false. Applied to the domain of religious discourse this works out as follows: 'God is omniscient' and 'God doesn't know everything' can both be true, even though the former proposition entails the denial of the latter. Or in another example: 'There is no salvation but through Christ's death and glorious resurrection' and 'humans work out their own salvation through the laws of karma and reincarnation' can both be true, even though the former proposition entails the falsity of the latter. But this way lies madness, *also* in the domain of religious discourse. If we reject bivalence in religious discourse and elsewhere, we legitimize nonsensical talk.[8]

And then there is this: it is an empirical fact that by far most religious people take bivalence for granted. That is why a Christian says that the Muslim is wrong in rejecting the doctrine of the Trinity – and a Muslim returns the compliment when he says that the Christian is wrong in accepting that doctrine.[9] The Muslim and the Christian hold incompatible beliefs about God. Someone who rejects bivalence must be willing to say that these incompatible beliefs can both be true. And it is an empirical fact that most Christians and most Muslims are not prepared to do that. The rejection of bivalence jeopardizes honest communication between adherents of different religions every bit as much as does the acceptance of pluralism. If, as Grube avers, pluralism sweeps serious religious differences under the carpet and thereby precludes honest communication, then the rejection of bivalence cannot be presented as a cure, for it equally sweeps serious religious differences under the carpet, and thereby also precludes honest communication.

An argument for religious toleration based on the rejection of bivalence, will have a paralyzing effect on every religious believer. For he is then urged to hold not only that his own religious beliefs are true but that someone else's beliefs that are incompatible with them, are true as well. And this, in turn, means that he is urged to hold that his beliefs are both true and false. These are the effects that the serious rejection of bivalence will work. But those effects are madness. Hence, if there is an argument for religious toleration, it better not be based on the rejection of bivalence.

## An epistemic argument for religious toleration?

After Grube has expressed allegiance to the rejection of bivalence, he offers an argument for toleration that does not rest on the rejection of bivalence! I now wish to examine his argument, the crucial notion of which is 'justification'. Now 'justification' is an epistemological term of art. When you ask a person in the street whether a particular belief of his is 'justified' he will be puzzled, as he has no clear idea what is being asked. Perhaps the best way to introduce the term is by giving examples, and then hope for the best. Someone living in the seventh century could not have been justified in believing that the earth revolves around the sun, even though it was already true in the seventh century that the earth revolves around the sun. So here we have truth without justification. But it is also possible to have justification without truth. For example: John Milton, let us suppose, believed that the Morning star and the Evening star are two different celestial bodies; his belief was justified but false. What these examples show is that truth and justification can come apart: a belief's truth does not entail that belief in it is justified, and the fact that a belief is justified does not entail that it is true.

Still, many epistemologists argue (or at least: hope), there is a relation between truth and justification.[10] Some have stated this relation as follows: the more justification you have for one of your beliefs, the more likely it is that that belief is true.[11]

This way of putting things indicates something else as well: justification is degree-sensitive. One person can have more justification for believing proposition p, than someone else. It brings out something else as well: justification, or the strength thereof, is person-relative. Suppose I heard via a usually unreliable source, *Bild* perhaps, that Bob broke his back; then, if I believe that Bob broke his back, my belief has much less justification than, say, you who shares my belief but were an eye witness to Bob's dismal fall from his horse. I assume that when Grube says that 'justification is plural' he means the same as what I have just said, viz. that justification is person-relative and degree-sensitive.

I said that 'justification' is the crucial notion in Grube's case for religious toleration. The case itself, or so it seems, is as follows: adherents of different world religions, Christians, Muslims, Jews, Hindus etc. surely believe different things – but their believing *attitudes*, given their respective epistemic circumstances, can all considered to be epistemically justified. And because they can all be so considered, adherents of the world's religions should be tolerant towards each other.

Earlier I added the qualifier 'or so it seems', because Grube nowhere makes his case for religious toleration fully explicit. In the opening section of his article he does explicitly say that he is going to offer a 'framework' that allows for religious toleration. The 'framework', as it turns out, just *is* the idea that adherents of the world's religions, given their different epistemic circumstances, are all epistemically justified in their religious beliefs. So I will take Grube upon his word: he does intend to offer an argument for religious toleration.[12] Hence, I take Grube's argument for religious toleration to run as follows:

(1) The adherents of the world's religions are justified in their religious beliefs.
(2) If the adherents of the world's religions are justified in their beliefs, they should be tolerated.
(3) Therefore, the adherents of the world's religions should be tolerated.

(And this entails that the adherents of the world's religions should tolerate each other.)

Is this argument convincing? It is at least puzzling for what it *does not* say. It does not say that religious toleration should be extended to people whose religious beliefs are *not* justified. For premise (2) formulates only a sufficient condition for toleration, not a necessary one. On the basis of this argument toleration can only be extended to persons whose religious beliefs are justified. If it is to be extended to persons whose beliefs are not justified, an additional argument is needed – an argument Grube has not offered. So, if his argument is successful, it at best offers a *partial* case for toleration. But is even the partial argument successful – is it plausible?

I am reluctant to say 'yes'. One reason is that, on the basis of what Grube has said about justification, I have no clue as to why we should think that premise (1) is true. Are adherents of the world's religions all epistemically justified in holding their religious beliefs? Well, what *is* justification? For all the work this notion is supposed to do for the argument, Grube leaves the reader in the dark as to when a person's belief is justified. He offers no conditions, neither necessary nor sufficient ones, that must be satisfied in order for someone's belief to be justified. Sure, he does say that the justificatory status of a person's belief depends 'on her perspective', 'on what information is available to her at a given moment', 'on her epistemological context', 'on her grounds', 'on whether she has carefully mustered the evidence', 'on the reasons she has for assuming her belief to be true' (422–423). And sure, he contrasts the notion of 'justification' with Wolterstorff's notion of 'entitlement' according to which a person is entitled to believe p if that person has fulfilled certain epistemic obligations. But these indications are radically insufficient to say with any assurance whether or not Christians (or any particular Christian), Muslims (or any particular Muslim) etc. in the contexts in which they happen to find themselves, are justified in their religious beliefs. A lot of recent epistemological discussion has gone into the question just what, if anything, justification *is* – and some have expressed grave doubts that there is one thing called 'justification'.[13] It bears pointing out that some accounts of justification are such that on their basis it could be argued that no one can be justified in her religious belief; other accounts are such that on their basis it could be argued that some but certainly not all religious believers can be justified in their beliefs; and yet other accounts are such that on their basis it could be argued that virtually all religious believers can. Let me give examples of each of these accounts.

Some accounts of justification have it that a person's belief is justified provided the belief is supported by scientifically validated methods of research. On this basis it has been argued that no one can be (and in fact no one is) justified in any religious belief she might have.[14]

Other accounts have it that a belief is justified provided the belief is produced by a de facto reliable belief-forming mechanism (and a belief-forming mechanism is reliable when the preponderance of beliefs formed by that mechanism are true).[15] On this account, someone may be justified in holding a belief without *knowing* that she is: that person's belief may be generated by a de facto reliable mechanism, without the person knowing that it is thus generated. On this basis it can be argued that if A's religious belief that p is generated by mechanism-1 and B's religious belief that not-p by mechanism-2, at least either A of B is not justified in her belief – and then either mechanism-1 or mechanism-2 must be unreliable.

Yet other accounts have it that a person is justified in holding a certain belief only if the degree of that person's belief is proportional to the degree to which it is probable given the evidence that is available to him.[16] In order to be able to address the questions whether a religious believer is justified in her belief, we need to know a lot about her evidence. In the absence of that, we cannot estimate whether she is justified in holding her belief.

On yet another account a person is justified in holding a belief provided her belief coheres with other beliefs that she holds.[17] If we do not know what other beliefs a person has, we cannot estimate whether a particular belief of her is justified.

All of this is goes to show that premise (1) of Grube's argument cannot be properly discussed unless we know a lot more about what Grube means by 'justification'. It also goes to show that whether one's religious belief will be counted as 'justified' is fully dependent on what one takes 'justification' to be.

What about premise (2)? Should we accept it? Again I am reluctant to say 'yes'. The worries I expressed about premise (1) carry over to (2) as well, of course. But (2) faces a new problem, even if my worry about what justification is would be alleviated. The problem is this: why should we even think that having a justified religious belief is *sufficient* for a believer to merit toleration? It would certainly seem possible that a person has a justified belief but still should not be tolerated. And this is something Grube himself acknowledges. Think of the quasi-religious Nazi-beliefs that some people have. These people should not be tolerated in this account.

So my question is: why should we even think there is a meaningful relation between a person's belief being justified, and that person's meriting toleration? As we have seen, near the end of his paper Grube himself admits that

(i) If a person's religious belief is *not* justified, that person may still merit toleration.

And he also admits that

(ii) Even if a person's religious belief *is* justified, that person may still *not* merit toleration.

Having admitted these points just is admitting that having justified belief is neither necessary nor sufficient for meriting toleration. And this means that there simply is no meaningful relation between justification and toleration. And this, in turn, means that we have not been given a solid argument for toleration.

To assess the plausibility of (2) in conjunction with the qualifications (i) and (ii), compare the following two statements that are mimicked after (2), (i) and (ii):

(2\*) If the adherents of the world's religions wear green shoes, they should be tolerated. [But (i) some adherents of the world's religions that don't wear green should also be tolerated; and (ii) some adherents of the world's religions that do wear green shoes should not be tolerated!]

(2\*\*) If the adherents of the world's religions are vegetarians, they should be tolerated. [But (i) some adherents of the world's religions that are not vegetarians should also be tolerated; and (ii) some vegetarian adherents of the world's religions should not be tolerated.]

(2\*) and (2\*\*), I take it, look silly. And they look silly because there just does not seem to be a meaningful relation between wearing green shoes and meriting toleration, nor a meaningful relation between being a vegetarian and meriting toleration. But (2) seems to be in the same league!

My conclusion of this section, then, is that we have not been given a successful argument for religious toleration on the basis of justified belief. Premise (1) needs a lot of work before it can be properly evaluated, whereas premise (2) as it stands is no more plausible than (2\*) or (2\*\*).[18]

**Notes**

1. Turner, *Tonight We Will Fake Love.*
2. Grube, "Justified Religious Difference."
3. Grube lumps together toleration and respect. These are, however, quite distinct attitudes. I may tolerate your views in the sense that Wolterstorff has explained, so in the sense that I take it upon me to put up with your beliefs that I thoroughly dislike. (Wolterstorff, "Tolerance, Justice, Dignity") But toleration does not require respect. In fact, it would seem that the more respect I have for your beliefs, the less occasion there is for me to have to tolerate your beliefs (or you). I therefore concentrate on toleration only.
4. See van Woudenberg, *Toeval en ontwerp in de wereld,* 153–68.
5. Grube subsumes under bivalence also the principle of excluded middle. But that is a different principle. Let 'Tp' represent 'p is true' and 'T-p' 'p is false' (and let 'v' represent the disjunction), then bivalence is Tp v T-p; excluded middle is T(p v-p). Since nothing in his argument hangs on this, I let it pass.
6. This is not to deny that in specific contexts sentences like the one given in de body of the text will usually have a determinate truth value: contextual clues indicate how the statement must be understood. Outside of any specific context, however, such sentences are incomplete.
7. Usually, bivalence is formulated in terms of propositions – and propositions are usually supposed to be meaningful, complete and unambiguous. See for example Audi, *Cambridge Dictionary of Philosophy,* s.v. 'Principle of Bivalence'.
8. In the Dutch context Jan Riemersma has recently also defended that bivalence should be given up, by arguing that true contradictions exist, i.e. that there are propositions such that both they and their denials are true. For an excellent response to this effort, see De Ridder, "Riemersma over Plantinga."
9. If two persons, say a Muslim and a Christian, have conflicting beliefs about God, this does not entail that they therefore refer to different Gods, or worship different Gods. Two persons can refer to the Dutch King, even if one of them believes he has three daughters, and the other that he has four. Likewise, two persons can refer to the only God that exists, but hold incompatible beliefs about God. See de Ridder & van Woudenberg, "Believing In, Referring To, and Worshipping the Same God."
10. See e.g. Lemos, *Introduction to the Theory of Knowledge,* 13–17.
11. E.g. BonJour, *Structure of Empirical Knowledge,* 7–8.
12. But I note that Grube's article seems to display shift of emphasis as it progresses: initially religious tolerance stands center stage, later on it is inter religious dialogue – which is quite another topic.
13. Alston, *Beyond 'Justification'.* As Peels 2010 argues, Alston's views are problematic. But what is not problematic is Alston's point that 'epistemic justification' is a moving target.
14. See Philipse, "The Real Conflict Between Science and Religion"; for a criticism of Philipse's proposal see Van Woudenberg & Rothuizen van der Steen, "Science and the Ethics of Belief."
15. Goldman, "What is Justified Belief"; Plantinga, *Warranted Christian Belief.*
16. Conee & Feldman, "Evidentialism."
17. Lehrer, *Theory of Knowledge,* 87.
18. For comments and advice on an earlier version of this paper, I am indebted to Kees van der Kooi, Rik Peels, and Jeroen de Ridder. Work on this paper was made possible by a grant from the Templeton World Charity Foundation; the views expressed in the paper are the author's and do not necessarily reflect the views of the grant-giver.

**Bibliography**

Alston, W. P. *Beyond 'Justification'. Dimensions of Epistemic Evaluation.* Ithaca, NY: Cornell University Press, 2005.

Audi, R. *The Cambridge Dictionary of Philosophy*. 3rd ed. Cambridge: Cambridge University Press, 2015.

BonJour, L. *The Structure of Empirical Knowledge*. Cambridge, MA: Harvard University Press, 1985.

de Ridder, J. "Riemersma over Plantinga: Een Weerlegging." *Radix* 39 (2013): 217–227.

de Ridder, J., and R. van Woudenberg. "Believing In, Referring To, and Worshipping the Same God. A Reformed View." *Faith and Philosophy* 31 (2014): 46–67. doi:10.5840/faithphil20141104.

Feldman, R., and E. Conee. "Evidentialism." *Philosophical Studies* 48 (1985): 15–34. doi:10.1007/BF00372404.

Goldman, A. "What is Justified Belief." In *Justification and Knowledge*, edited by G. S. Pappas, 1–23. Dordrecht: Reidel, 1979.

Grube, D.-M. "Justified Religious Difference. A Constructive Approach to Religious Diversity." *The International Journal of Philosophy and Theology* 76 (2015): 419–427.

Lehrer, K. *Theory of Knowledge*. London: Routledge, 1990.

Lemos, N. *An Introduction to the Theory of Knowledge*. Cambridge: Cambridge University Press, 2007.

Peels, R. "Epistemic Desiderata and Epistemic Pluralism." *Journal of Philosophical Research* 35 (2010): 193–207. doi:10.5840/jpr_2010_7.

Philipse, H. "The Real Conflict Between Science and Religion: Alvin Plantinga's *Ignoratio Elenchis*." *European Journal for Philosophy of Religion* 5 (2013): 87–110.

Plantinga, A. *Warranted Christian Belief*. Oxford: Oxford University Press, 2000.

Turner, S. *Tonight We Will Fake Love*. London: Razor Book, 1978.

Van Woudenberg, R. *Toeval en ontwerp in de wereld. Apologetische analyses*. Budel: Damon, 2003.

Van Woudenberg, R., and J. Rothuizen-van der Steen. "Science and the Ethics of Belief. An Examination of Philipse's Rule 'R'." *Journal for the General Philosophy of Science* (2016). doi:10.1007/s10838-015-9313-9.

Wolterstorff, N. "Tolerance, Justice, Dignity." *The International Journal of Philosophy and Theology* 76 (2015): 377–386.

# Grube on justified religious difference

Vincent Brümmer

This paper is a response to Dirk-Martin Grube's article elsewhere in this issue. After discussing the points on which I agree with Grube, I explain why his notion of bivalence has not yet received the accuracy it needs.

Dirk-Martin Grube's article published elsewhere in this issue is clearly argued and thought provoking. I am especially pleased with his attempt to provide theological reasons for inter-religious tolerance and against the 'paternalistic' attitude with which many religious believers look down on other religious traditions than their own. This attitude is not only found among religious believers, but also with atheists like Richard Dawkins who characterises atheists as the 'brights' and all religious believers as intellectually inferior and misguided.

Tolerance (like intolerance) is an *anti*-attitude in the sense that I can only be tolerant towards views with which I *disagree*. I do not tolerate views with which I agree – I affirm them. Thus, Grube correctly emphasises that inter-religious tolerance entails acknowledgement and respect for the *otherness* of other religious traditions. Such tolerance also entails an open attitude in which we try not only to understand the other's beliefs in their otherness but also, as Grube puts it, to 'mirror' our own beliefs in those of others in the sense that we can try to learn from them. We cannot learn from beliefs which are identical with our own but only from those that differ from ours.

Grube admits that there are limits to such inter-religious tolerance. Sometimes adherents to other religious traditions (and also to our own Christian tradition!) adhere to beliefs and practices which we consider dangerous and unjustifiable. We are unwilling to respect or tolerate such beliefs and practices. Grube points out that at this point we require criteria for distinguishing between justified and unjustified beliefs and practices, between those that we are willing to respect and tolerate and those that we consider intolerable. Although Grube does not deal with this issue in his lecture, he notes that this is on his agenda for the future. I look forward to see what criteria he will recommend as relevant in this regard.

I can also agree with Grube's critique of the way in which religious pluralists like Paul Knitter and John Hick try to defend mutual respect and tolerance between adherents of different religions. As Grube puts it, 'their guiding intention is to minimise or neutralise the differences between different religions. To that end, they postulate some kind of unity between the different religions' (420). This kind of pluralism fails on two points. First of all, in trying 'to minimise and neutralise the differences' it fails to do justice to the other tradition *in its otherness*. As I stated above, I agree with Grube that respect for the otherness of the other is not only a logically necessary condition for the possibility of toleration as such but also essential for taking the views of the other seriously and for the possibility to 'mirror' one's own beliefs in those of the other. Second, it is not enough to merely *postulate* in an *a priori* fashion that there is 'some kind of unity between different religions.' Whether or not different religious traditions overlap is a matter for empirical investigation. It can only be the outcome of a careful comparison between the beliefs and practices of different religious traditions. This applies especially to the claim that all religions share a common core. This may or may not be the case, but we cannot merely assume that it is. It could of course be argued that all religions try to provide answers to the same fundamental *questions* about life and the world. This is the reason for calling them all 'religions.' However, we cannot merely assume that their *answers* will overlap or share a common core. They may share the questions, but in the end they differ in the answers they provide.

Although I can wholeheartedly agree with much of Grube's argument in his lecture, there is one point about which I have some doubts, namely his rejection of what he calls the principle of 'bivalence.' He defines this as 'a logical principle which implies that statements have exactly one and not more than one truth value. They are *either* true *or* false. A logic satisfying this principle is called a two-valued or bivalent logic. For today's purposes I subsume the negative formulation of bivalence, the law of excluded middle, under biva-lence. Bivalence understood in this sense ... implies that, if position A is true and position B differs from A, B *must* be false. ... I summarise this point by suggesting that bivalence implies an *equation between difference and falsehood*' (421; emphasis in original).

Contrary to Grube, I hold that the law of excluded middle states an essential require-ment for the possibility of making any statement at all, or more generally, for the success of any legitimate speech act. However, the law of excluded middle is not what Grube calls bivalence. Grube's principle of bivalence 'implies that if position A is true and position B differs from A, B *must* be false.' This is not what the law of excluded middle states, nor is it true. If my statement 'that the object is green' is true, your statement 'that the object is large' is *different* from mine, but is not thereby necessarily *false*. Your statement would only be false if it *contradicts* my statement and not merely when it is *different* from mine. To use Grube's formulation, the law of excluded middle does not imply 'an equation between *difference* and falsity' but 'an equation between *logical contradiction* and falsity.'

Grube explains his rejection of the principle of 'bivalence' by means of the following example. 'Say, person A explains the aggressive attitude Germany took right before the First World War in purely materialistic terms. Maybe she suggests that it wished to expand its overseas colonies. Person B, however, may explain this attitude in non-materialistic terms, say, by suggesting that Germans and especially their emperor suffered from minority complexes since Germany was not recognised as a pear among the then-leading nations in Europe' (423). According to Grube, both these explanations can be justified although the beliefs implied in them differ. 'Persons A and B can *both* be justified to hold different beliefs on the same issue. Thus, a plurality of different beliefs can be legitimate' (423). The point is that these two explanations can both be true because, although they are different, they do not contradict each other. This is similar to saying that the object is both green and large, because these two assertions do not contradict each other, even though they are different.

But what is the nature of the difference between Grube's persons A and B? I think that we should distinguish here between two senses in which we use the term 'cause.' Sometimes we mean the 'complete cause' and other times we mean '*the* cause' or 'the most important or significant cause.' The complete cause includes all the necessary conditions which jointly are sufficient to bring about an event or state of affairs. Since each of these conditions presupposes further necessary condition, etc., the complete cause includes an infinite number of conditions. Usually, however, we consider one of more of these conditions as *the* cause of the event in the sense of the most important, or significant cause, or the one that we hold responsible or to which we ascribe praise or blame. Like Grube's persons A and B, we can differ about which of the conditions we consider to be *the* cause. This point can be explained with a nice example that I derive from John R. Lucas (*Freedom and Grace*, 1976): The coroner will say the cause of death was drowning, the unsuccessful rescuer will think the cause was his failure to dive well enough, the teenage chum will know that it was his folly in having dared his friend to swim to the wreck, the mother that it was having let him go out to swim on such a nasty cold day, the father that it was having failed to instil more sense and more moral courage into his head. All these explanations may be true because, although different, they do not contradict each other and can all be truly part of the complete cause. The considerations upon which we decide which of the necessary conditions is to count as *the* cause of an event, are complex and in different circumstances different considerations will be relevant. It is not possible to discuss these considerations in detail here. However, the important point here is that the difference between Grube's persons A and B is not one of truth but of importance or significance. It is not an epistemic difference but one of judgement.

I can agree that the differences between religious traditions include such differences in judgement. However, religious traditions differ in many other ways as well, including differences in the epistemic claims they make. In many respects, they are not merely different but they also contradict each other. In such cases, the law of excluded middle decrees that they cannot all be equally true or equally justified.

**Bibliography**

Grube, D.-M. "Justified Religious Difference: A Constructive Approach to Religious Diversity." *International Journal of Philosophy and Theology* 76, no. 5 (2015): 419–427.

# Response to Dirk-Martin Grube

Sami Pihlström

This paper responds to an essay by Dirk-Martin Grube published in this same journal issue. Special attention is drawn to issues such as tolerance, respect, and the recognition of otherness regarding religious beliefs. Grube interestingly suggests that the focus on religious truth should be replaced by a focus on justification. Some critical remarks on these suggestions are made.

Dirk-Martin Grube's reflections on what he calls 'justified religious difference' in his article in this journal issue are most welcome in a world in which conflicts, including violent conflicts, between religious (and, for that matter, non-religious) people and groups are with us to stay. Insofar as academic philosophy of religion today can be expected not only to enhance our theoretical understanding of religious belief and religious language-use in purely intellectual contexts but also to serve our societies by supporting the peaceful coexistence of different religious outlooks, there can hardly be a more vital task for philosophers of religion than the one of developing views allowing for 'tolerance and respect for religions other than [one's] home religion' (419).[1]

Let me point out right away that I am in many ways fundamentally in agreement with Grube. I also share his basically pragmatist approach in the philosophy of religion (which is not as explicit in the essay to be commented upon here as in some of his other works, though). Therefore, I will try to focus, in this response paper, on some formulations in his essay that raise my doubts or that I at least feel ought to be somehow reformulated. I will sound much more critical than I really am, because the general context of this criticism is our overall agreement. I am deeply grateful for this opportunity to continue discussing key issues in the philosophy of religion with Dirk-Martin Grube by offering my brief critical response to his essay.

The simple-sounding plea for *tolerance* and *respect* already leads us to a question. Clearly, tolerance and respect are very different notions. One may tolerate something while not respecting it – indeed, while not respecting it at all. For example, we may find it necessary to tolerate, in the name of the morally and politically fundamental principle of the freedom of thought and speech in liberal societies, some extremist religious groups – presumably only to the extent that they refrain from using violence against others (though even this may be a problematic line to draw, as we know very well that such groups might use at least psychological if not physical violence against, for example, their own dissident or potentially dissident members) – while not respecting their activities that conflict with our liberal values. We may, and presumably should, be willing to let individuals and groups develop their own religious outlooks as freely as possible, at least to the extent that others' freedom to do so is not violated, but it does not follow that all those outlooks ought to be treated with equal respect. Tolerance, then, is significantly weaker than respect. Conversely, we may, and should, be suspicious of someone who says, for instance, that s/he 'tolerates' refugees. A populist right-wing politician could easily utter words like that. This would be a morally thin relation to adopt to people seeking an asylum and fleeing war and poverty; in civilized societies, refugees should obviously be granted not only tolerance but appropriate respect.

Some philosophers and theologians have tried to develop a notion that falls in between mere tolerance on the one hand and the considerably stronger attitude of full acceptance (or full respect), on the other hand – while being perhaps closer to respect than to tolerance. This is the notion of *recognition* (*Anerkennung*), or as some others prefer to label it, *acknowledgment*. Granting recognition to someone, or some group, is not merely to tolerate that person or group but to affirm more strongly her/his/its positive value while still possibly disagreeing with her/him/it even in some fundamental respect. Grube does not develop this conceptual machinery in his essay, and here I cannot deal with the matter in any detail, but certainly the relations between notions like tolerance, respect, and recognition deserve further attention.[2]

In his search for philosophical articulations of tolerance and respect for otherness, Grube is not satisfied with John Hick's 'pluralism', according to which different religions are in touch with the same transcendent reality (420). The problem with such a view, he argues, is basically the same as in Immanuel Kant's notion of the *Ding an sich*. Nothing meaningful can be said about the relation between the transcendent reality that all empirical religions are supposed to be about and those empirical religions themselves (420). What Grube might do at this point is to pause to consider whether an analogy to the so-called one world reading of Kant's distinction between things in themselves and appearances[3] would be helpful in this context. Would the idea of empirical religions' being in some meaningful relation to the transcendent 'Real *an sich*' be easier to develop in this interpretive framework than in the more traditional one postulating two 'worlds', the noumenal and the phenomenal?

Be that as it may, it might also be asked whether a more *pragmatic* version of pluralism – operating at the meta-level – would be relevant here. Perhaps it is not just the different religions themselves that should be regarded as the basic units of a pluralism seeking to overcome their apparent differences (as in Hick's case); perhaps the relevant kind of pluralism functions at the level of philosophical views concerning the ways in which religions and/or theologies take themselves to be related to the ultimately real. This type of pluralism in the philosophy of religion could be based on, for example, William James's pragmatism; it would, in fact, be very different from the Hickian pluralism Grube rightly criticizes.[4] I would be willing to argue (though again this matter cannot be settled here) that a pragmatic form of pluralism has much better chances to avoid 'losing sight of the religious Other *in her Otherness*' (421) than Hick's more straightforward religious pluralism.

After having set aside Hick's pluralism, Grube moves on to a positive articulation of his own approach. One important background idea here is the rejection of the principle of *bivalence*, according to which statements are either true or false (without any third option). Applied to the issue of 'other religions', the principle of bivalence entails that we must regard religious statements differing from our own as false. However, I am not fully convinced that we need to go as far as this. Couldn't one just hold on to a bivalent logic while sincerely admitting that one's own beliefs might be false? This would be to endorse general fallibilism about one's beliefs, religious beliefs included, and there is no reason why such intellectual and theological humility would necessarily conflict with bivalence as a logical principle.

It is, I think, another matter entirely to admit that in discussing features of human culture generally – religion, art, politics, philosophy, etc. – it may be extremely difficult or impossible to formulate clearly bivalently true or false statements about complex cultural matters (6). But this, again, can be admitted without giving up the principle of bivalence itself. We only need to pay attention to where exactly that principle is relevant. Furthermore, the rejection of bivalence easily leads to self-reflective problems. Grube writes: 'There is thus more than only the bivalent pair of truth values, "true" and "false". There is a third one, "indeterminate", and there are probably more' (421). Is he here making bivalently true or false meta-level statements about bivalence and truth-values, or could these statements themselves be something indeterminate?

Grube does not simply base his reflections on the rejection of bivalence, either, although he finds it an important starting point. He proposes to focus on *justification* rather than truth, thus going 'beyond the realm of logic and truth altogether' (421–422). This again sounds to me like a slight exaggeration. Focusing on justification is certainly not going beyond logic and truth, as justification must be tied to truth in some relevant sense (though it may be debatable how exactly). We are told that justification differs from truth because it is attributed to agents holding beliefs, rather than to the beliefs held (422). Well, I think it is common to speak of beliefs (as well as methods of forming beliefs) being justified or unjustified. Does Grube mean that this is always indirectly a way of speaking about the agents of those beliefs? But what if we want to refer to, for example, possible justifications for beliefs that no one actually holds, that is, if we cannot identify any agent to speak about? Or if we speak about beliefs held collectively, such as beliefs that are part of the 'scientific worldview', whatever that ultimately comes down to, or part of some collectively affirmed religious creed that no individual agent might literally stick to? Do we then have to postulate a collective agent 'holding' that belief?

It is also problematic, in my view, to maintain that 'justification kicks in only where truth is uncertain' (422). The example Grube uses here is racism. The racist could base her/his beliefs upon 'obviously false assumptions', in which case 'the question whether he is justified to hold his beliefs does not arise' (422). I suppose in most cases of real political and ethical (or religious) controversies, this may be precisely what is really at stake: it may be hard to determine that a person, or a group, relies on obviously false assumptions. This is of course easier in the case of racism than in some more advanced political debates, but often the debate concerns the justifiability of those assumptions themselves. In short, it is not easy – it may actually be impossible – to draw a clear line between the facts about which every rational person agrees and the valuational or normative claims that are independent of those facts and may therefore be disputable. My worry here is that Grube's approach may be based on a version of the fact/value dichotomy that he (as a pragmatist) might find good reasons to oppose.[5] The notion of 'obviously false assumptions' might not be as easily available in real-life religious conflicts as the relatively easy example of racism can lead us to think.

More positively, one of Grube's key ideas here is that justification is *context- and perspective-dependent* in a manner different from truth. A plurality of different beliefs could be legitimate (justified), given the different contexts in which the agents holding those beliefs operate (422–423). It is easy to agree with this suggestion, but it should also be pointed out that there is no reason to think this would harm the principle of bivalence. Those context-sensitive beliefs would not necessarily have to run into conflict with each other within a bivalent logic.

This leads us to my more general worries about Grube's position. If we want to maintain an attitude that 'acknowledges genuine Otherness' by acknowledging that others' beliefs (different from mine) 'are nevertheless justified' (423), aren't we running the risk of sliding into something like *radical relativism*? An easy way to avoid such an outcome would be to admit merely that others' beliefs (different from mine) *could be* justified, not that they *are*. The other could, after all, be in a problematic epistemic context, yet unable to recognize those problems from within that very context. In fact, a couple of pages later Grube much more carefully says that 'you can be justified in holding your […] beliefs, given *your* epistemic circumstances, while I can be simultaneously justified in holding my Christian beliefs, given *my* epistemic circumstances' (424). This still leaves it open whether the other actually is justified in holding her/his beliefs – or whether I am.

Grube importantly distinguishes between the open-minded attitude acknowledging genuine otherness from the opposed attitude postulating an 'intellectual *monopoly*' and claiming 'principled cognitive privileges' (423). He is certainly right to attack the 'new atheists' (e.g., Richard Dawkins) for succumbing to the temptations of the latter kind of attitude. However, in addition to the worry that being *too* open-minded might open the door for relativism, one might also ask whether this basic distinction between open-mindedness and alleged cognitive privilege is itself dependent on a problematically bivalent logic. One could claim that these attitudes are contraries rather than contradictories. There could, then, be a middle path option available – an attitude that does not acknowledge others' beliefs as justified too simply and straightforwardly but is prepared to subordinate them (as well as one's own beliefs) to critical scrutiny, albeit in a manner taking seriously their context-sensitivity (as well as that of one's own beliefs).

All of this is ultimately connected with the 'tolerance and respect' theme Grube's essay opens with. Tolerance and respect, he tells us, do not require similarity to one's 'home-religion' but 'depend on the knowledge that the religious Other can be justified to hold her deviant religious beliefs coupled with the assurance that this knowledge does not jeopardize the legitimacy of the home religion' (424). This is fine as far as it goes, but very soon Grube again switches from modal formulations ('can') to indicative ones: 'An important consequence of the knowledge that the Other is justified in holding the religious beliefs she holds is respect for her religious Otherness' (425). How can we *know* that the Other *is* justified in holding her beliefs? Is it, more generally, necessary to speak about knowledge here at all? We could acknowledge the possibility that the others' beliefs are justified (or our own beliefs false) without claiming to know this to be the case.

Fortunately, Grube explicitly recognizes the dangers of relativism (referring briefly to Jacques Derrida, whose commitment to relativism is hardly clear, though) and urges us not to 'ignore the *limits* of tolerating Otherness' (425). However, we are told relatively little about how exactly those limits are to be drawn. This, of course, is something that Grube himself recognizes, too, pointing out that we need to develop criteria that allow us to distinguish between justified and unjustified beliefs (426). Here we are merely provided the assurance that the framework of 'justified religious difference' will be able to – or is even 'particularly well-equipped' to – deal with this matter and with accounting for some religious beliefs being unjustified or illegitimate.

I suppose Grube would at this point be willing to rely on his basic pragmatist commitments and seek to draw the distinction between justified and unjustified beliefs in some practice-involving way, for example, by referring to the different ways in which our religious (or non-religious) beliefs could, or could fail to, contribute to the good life or to human overall satisfactoriness. William James's pragmatist philosophy of religion, as developed in *The Varieties of Religious Experience* (1902) and *Pragmatism* (1907), in particular, would be helpful here.[6] We need to look at Grube's other writings – more explicitly addressing pragmatist philosophy of religion – in order to find out how exactly he employs pragmatism (or pragmatic pluralism) in dealing with this problem. Hence, further inquiries into this matter are beyond this response paper. It must be noted, however, that adopting the Jamesian line here would also require us to *soften the distinction between justification and truth* – which might then raise further questions regarding the coherence of Grube's position.

## Notes

1. I will cite Dirk-Martin Grube's essay by providing the page numbers in the text. The emphases, unless otherwise indicated, are in the original.
2. In modern philosophy, the discussion of recognition basically starts from Axel Honneth's, Charles Taylor's, and Nancy Fraser's seminal contributions (largely indebted to Hegel). The Faculty of Theology at the University of Helsinki currently hosts an Academy of Finland 'Centre of Excellence' on 'Reason and Religious Recognition' (2014–2019), led by Risto Saarinen (with Dirk-Martin Grube as one of its international collaborators); in this comprehensive research unit, the concept of recognition is extensively studied in relation to theology and philosophy of religion. Saarinen's own book manuscript, *Recognition in Religion*, explores the matter in historical detail. The concept of acknowledgment, on the other hand, is more widely used in the Wittgensteinian context developed in, for example, Cavell, *The Claim of Reason*. For my own brief attempt to emphasize the difference between recognition and acknowledgment in relation to the problem of evil in the philosophy of religion, see Pihlström, *Taking Evil Seriously*.
3. As defended, for example, in Allison, *Kant's Transcendental Idealism*.
4. Cf., for example, Pihlström, *Pragmatic Pluralism*.
5. See, for example, Putnam, *The Collapse of the Fact/Value Dichotomy*.
6. Both classical works by James are available in *The Works of William James*. Cf. Pihlström, *Pragmatic Pluralism*.

## Bibliography

Allison, H. E. *Kant's Transcendental Idealism: An Interpretation and Defense. Revised and Enlarged Edition.* 1st ed. 1983. Reprint, New Haven, CT: Yale University Press, 2004.
Cavell, S. *The Claim of Reason.* New York, NY: Oxford University Press, 1979.
Grube, D.-M. "Justified Religious Difference. A Constructive Approach to Religious Diversity." *International Journal of Philosophy and Theology* 76, no. 5 (2015): 419–427.

James, W. *The Works of William James*. edited by Frederick H. Burkhardt, Fredson Bowers, and Ignas K. Skrupskelis. Cambridge, MA: Harvard University Press, 1975–88.

Pihlström, S. *Pragmatic Pluralism and the Problem of God*. New York, NY: Fordham University Press, 2013.

Pihlström, S. *Taking Evil Seriously*. Basingstoke: Palgrave, 2014.

Putnam, H. *The Collapse of the Fact/Value Dichotomy and Other Essays*. Cambridge, MA: Harvard University Press, 2002.

Saarinen, R. *Recognition and Religion*. Book ms., forthcoming.

# What about unjustified religious difference? Response paper to Dirk-Martin Grube's 'justified religious difference'

Peter Jonkers

The aim of this paper is to shed some light on the distinction between justified and unjustified religious diversity, a problem that Dirk-Martin Grube only hinted at in his article '*Justified Religious Difference*.' This article's focus is not so much on the epistemological question of justifying religious difference, but on how to deal with it in the societal sphere. This implies that religions and religious diversity will be approached from a practical perspective, that is, as (reasoned) ways of life. I start by examining the opportunities and problems of religious diversity, opposing a universalist and a particularist view on this issue. Religious difference is an opportunity, because it is intertwined with creativity and innovation, but it is also a problem, because it confronts us with incompatible judgments, irreconcilable values, and contrary principles. Notwithstanding the legitimate objections that can be raised against the particularist position, the above observations seriously undermine Grube's idea that the distinction between justified and unjustified religious difference can be made unambiguously, because of the heterogeneous character of the idea of justification itself. In order to deal with this issue, I propose a re-examination of the idea of tolerance, defined as a virtue: I disapprove of your manner of living, but I respect in it your liberty to live as you please and I recognize your right to manifest it publicly. But this virtue makes only sense against the background of the intolerable, which is the translation of the idea of unjustified religious difference into the language of the public debate. This idea serves as an always fragile limit to tolerance.

## 1. Introduction

In his article,[1] Dirk-Martin Grube offers a defense of justified religious difference, a question that is not only hotly debated by contemporary philosophers of religion but also in the public debate on religious pluralism in general. In Grube's view, an epistemological justification of the current divergence of religious convictions not only offers a theoretical framework for dealing with religious diversity in a constructive way but also fosters, on a practical level, an attitude of tolerance and respect with regard to the religious other. In my response, I will, just like Grube, discuss the question of religious diversity from a philosophical perspective, but leave his treatment of the epistemological aspects of this question, especially of the principle of bivalence, aside. I will rather concentrate on the question how to deal with religious diversity in the societal sphere, thereby questioning whether the distinction between justified and unjustified religious difference can be made as unambiguously as Grube suggests. Admittedly, my societal and cultural approach of religious diversity is first of all a matter of personal interest, but I am also convinced that it is essential for philosophy of religion to link its traditional (epistemological, hermeneutical, metaphysical, etc.) ways of thinking about religion and God to the burning questions about the ways, in which religions appear in the public space.

The main aim of this paper is to show the problematic nature of a sharp distinction between justified and unjustified religious diversity. At the end of his text, Grube states that he concentrated on justified religious difference, because dealing with unjustified religious diversity would have required him to develop criteria to make the distinction between these two kinds of religious diversity, which was more than he could do in his article. Although it would indeed be unfair to expect that one single paper could answer all the thorny questions regarding religious diversity, I think that the question of how to distinguish between justified and unjustified religious difference is one of the most urgent ones of our time, and is directly linked to the even more pressing question of (religious) tolerance. It goes far beyond the fact that justification itself is plural, a matter that Grube discusses extensively in his paper. Furthermore, my response to Grube's article approaches religions and religious diversity from a practical perspective: this means to interpret religions not so much from a doctrinal perspective, but as (reasoned) ways of life. Furthermore, an investigation into the nature of religious diversity should not take the ideal situation of a cordial dialogue between Christian, Muslim and Jewish friends about the (dis)similarities between the three great religions of the Book as its (paradigmatic) starting point, but rather start from the reality of concrete (conflicting) practices that follow from the current large diversity of ways of life.[2] Limiting the discussion on beforehand to the unproblematic aspects of religious diversity takes the sting out of the debate and circumvents the enormous theoretical and practical problems that immediately crop up when questioning the distinction between justified and unjustified religious diversity.

## 2. The problems and opportunities of religious diversity

As a starting point, I take Grube's critique of (religious) pluralism. In addition to his criticisms on empirical (finding a common core for religious pluralism is a tour de force) and theoretical (since the postulate of the *Real an sich* as the hidden core of all religions is unfathomable, it is unable to qualify any empirical religion) grounds, I want to draw the attention to the problematic consequences of religious pluralism from a practical perspective, that is, from the point of view of people's concrete religious (ritual, ethical, and customary) practices. Religions differ in their teachings about a truly fulfilled life, after which their adherents are striving. But religious diversity typically does not become conflictual on a doctrinal level, for the simple reason that this only matters to a very limited group of people, viz. religious leaders, theologians, and philosophers of religion. Instead, conflicts over religious diversity arise when these doctrines are translated into concrete practices, thus colliding with the practical translations of other teachings. Well, just like Hick tried to solve the theological problem of religious diversity by postulating the *Real an sich*, which was meant to serve as a common, but hidden point of reference for the doctrines of all religions, Hans Küng introduced the idea of a world ethos as a means to settle the (practical) conflicts arising from religious diversity in a peaceful way: 'No survival without world ethic. No world peace without peace between the religions. No peace between the religions without dialogue between the religions.'[3]

To my mind, Küng's solution of the problematic consequences of religious diversity on a practical level raises the same problems as Hick's solution of the theoretical or doctrinal ones. In general, religious diversity presents both an opportunity and a problem. It is an opportunity because diversity is intertwined with creativity and innovation, but it is also a problem, because it confronts us with incompatible judgments, irreconcilable values, and contrary principles, thus easily leading to conflicts. As said, the conflictual consequences of religious diversity become apparent when religious doctrines are translated into concrete practices, especially when (the official representatives of) the religions that prescribe these practices are asked to justify themselves.[4] Küng, just like many other universalists, thinks that it is both possible and desirable to search for universal moral principles that are valid independently of the religions that apply them. In his view, this search eventually leads to a kind of global/universal ethic that unifies all major religious (and secular) ways of life, and is based on the basic principles of right and wrong of human behavior and the principles to put them into action. Küng's ambitious project resulted in the Declaration of a Global Ethic (passed in 1993), in which 'people of very different religious backgrounds for the first time agreed on a minimum of irrevocable directives which they were already affirming in their own traditions.'[5] This declaration is based on the positive phrasing of the Golden Rule ('what you wish done to yourself, do to others'), and includes the ideals of a culture without violence with respect for all forms of life, of solidarity with a just economic order, of tolerance and trustworthiness, and of equal rights and partnership of women and men.[6] This shows that Küng's idea of a world ethos as a way to solve the problematic consequences of religious diversity on a practical level is quite similar to Hick's idea of the *Real an sich*, as an epistemological solution to the problem of religious pluralism.

I agree with Grube that Hick's idea of pluralism rests on the postulate of an underlying unity or common ground (the *Real an sich*). This postulate causes all kinds of epistemological problems: either it downplays religious diversity as such or it denounces the other's religious convictions as simply false, insofar as they cannot be integrated in this underlying unity. Grube argues that this is so, because the postulate of the *Real an sich* is coupled with the principle of bivalence: if one religious position is true, the other must be false. When we turn our attention to religions (and secular world views) as practical ways of life, the idea of a global ethic or a world ethos, meant to serve as a unifying postulate of religious pluralism, is problematic on similar grounds: since this postulate is incapable to bridge the gap between the abstract level of the general ethical principles and the concrete reality of diverging (religious) practices, it risks to downplay these differences or denounce them insofar as they cannot be integrated in the world ethos. If the practical consequences of religious diversity give rise to conflicts between the adherents of various religions, what is at stake is not so much the golden rule, being the underlying principle of the world ethic, but irreconcilable, very concrete practices, such as the rules for social intercourse (e.g., the role of women in the public sphere), ritual practices (Sunday's rest, killing animals without anesthesia), and ethical obligations (in particular about beginning and end of life issues). In sum, the main reasons that this trans-religious world ethics has fallen short of expectations are that the richness and concreteness of the various religious traditions is lost, and that the latter's 'thick' ethics is replaced by a 'thin' one, which shows, moreover, a rather Western anthropocentric character.[7]

Against this background, it is no surprise that the project of a trans-religious ethics is rejected by people who can be labelled as 'particularists.' They defend the view that each culture and religion has its own particular values and norms, which are incommensurable with those of other cultures and religions. This leads inevitably to the view that morality is relative to culture, and that what is right or wrong will vary according to cultural norms. Hence, the beliefs and values and cultural habits of other people should be respected unreservedly, and there should be no attempts to change or interfere in foreign traditions.[8] The problematic consequences of this particularist position are not only that they deprive the concepts of truth and morality of their normative functions, as Grube argues, but also that the distinction between justified and unjustified religious diversity becomes completely pointless. The reason for this is that not only the substance of all our concrete ways of life, including the traditions and values we cherish, is thus reduced to the level of cultural contingencies but also that what counts as justification becomes dependent on one's cultural environment. Without going as far as to say that every belief is as good as every other, which is a silly and self-refuting kind of relativism,[9] the inevitable consequence of the particularist view is that not only the concept of truth but also that of justification are replaced by the idea of plausibility in a given (and hence local) community.

## 3. Unjustified religious diversity and the idea of tolerance

Notwithstanding the legitimate objections that can be raised against some of the consequences of the particularist position, in particular the incommensurability of different religious beliefs, the least one can say is that it seriously undermines Grube's core idea of justified religious difference. According to this view, religious diversity is a consequence of people's different religious perspectives and different epistemological contexts, but it leaves the idea of justification intact: a Christian can accept the Jewish, Islamic, Buddhist, Hindu, etc., belief of others, because she knows that they can be *justified* to hold their deviant beliefs, and this knowledge does not jeopardize her justification to continue holding her Christian beliefs. In sum, according to Grube, justified religious difference provides the opportunity to pursue the interreligious dialogue in an open spirit, without being tempted to reduce religious diversity to (marginal) manifestations of an underlying unity, as Hick does. But although Grube's suggestion is sympathetic to me, because it supports the respect of the religious other, I don't think that it is able to solve the problem of the justification of religious diversity. To phrase it a bit polemically, he confines the respect of the religious other to the people who have divergent religious convictions on grounds that are, in his eyes, justified or at least justifiable, and he refers to his dialogues with his Muslim and Jewish friends as concrete examples of the fruitfulness of such an approach. But how to relate to people, who have different religious views and (above all) practices on unjustified grounds, that is, whom Grube cannot respect because their ways of life are objectionable or even repulsive? To my mind, the problem of bivalence, which he tried to discard in his paper, here returns on a more principled level. Grube rightfully rejects bivalence, because it proved to be unhelpful for the justification of religious diversity; instead he proposes justified religious diversity as a more open-minded and positive way to deal with the religious other. But this leaves the question unanswered if and how can he avoid a bivalent logic or, phrased positively, be just as open-minded and positive toward people who hold religious beliefs that are, in his eyes, *unjustified*. And, more importantly, can he convincingly show that he can make such a distinction without imposing his own criteria of justification upon others, and, consequently, being accused of a biased view on the really (because not meeting the criteria of justification) religious other? As I tried to point out through my practical approach of religion and religious diversity as conflicting ways of life, these questions are anything but speculative, but dominate the current public debate about religious diversity.

Let us examine the problem of the justification of religious diversity on a more fundamental level. According to Grube, whether a person is justified to hold a belief depends to a good extent on the epistemological circumstances she happens to be in, so that justification becomes plural: persons A and B can *both* be justified to hold different beliefs on the same issue, and, hence, deserve to be equally respected in holding these beliefs. But, at the same time Grube holds on to the homogeneous nature of the process of justification: an agent is justified in holding a belief because she has acquired it in epistemologically praiseworthy ways, for example, by carefully mustering the available evidence. Grube thereby refers to Clifford's classical example under which conditions a ship-owner is justified to believe that his ship is seaworthy. But while this homogeneity does not cause major difficulties when mustering empirical data, it raises insurmountable problems when religious beliefs are at stake. These problems are not only theoretical, resulting from the fact that religious beliefs are about the supernatural, but also practical, in the sense that a religious way of life can only justify itself, that is, by living it, not by referring to an external, objective reality. In sum, although Grube's idea of justification certainly allows for religious difference, it nevertheless still hinges on the homogeneous character of the empirical evidence that has to be mustered for religious beliefs in order to qualify as justified. However, in my view, the real problem of religious diversity has to do with the fact that these differences are not situated in a homogeneous, but in a hetero-geneous frame of reference. This heterogeneity not only implies religious diversity, as Grube argues, but also affects the very concept of justification, thus making it impossible to distinguish unambiguously between justified and unjustified religious diversity.

So the fundamental question, which is central in the ongoing public debate, is how to deal with religious diversity in a context of heterogeneity, that is, when making a clear-cut distinction between justified and unjustified, religious difference has become problematic. It has to be noted beforehand that heterogeneity is not identical with incommensurability, which would make a reasonable discussion about religious difference pointless a priori. As we all know, there are many forms of unjustified and even unjustifiable religious difference, especially on a practical level, and it is essential to respond to them in a reasonable, that is, non-decisionist way. This takes me to the issue of religious tolerance.[10] To my mind, the question of tolerance completely loses its sting, if it is reduced to those expressions of religious diversity, which I (or the community to which I belong) find justified or, at least, acceptable. The Latin word 'tolerare' originally means bearing a burden, implying that tolerance is about enduring a situation or behavior that one disagrees with on principled grounds. This meaning contrasts quite sharply with how tolerance appears in the public debate of our times.[11] In fact, today's society seems to have become so tolerant with regard to religious and other kinds of diversity that it even is considered as politically incorrect to criticize, let alone object to the deviant ideas and practices of others. In fact, all religious differences have become indifferent, thereby making the distinction between justified and unjustified religious diversity completely obsolete. This attitude can be summarized as: 'I approve of all ways of life, as long as they do not manifestly harm third parties; in short, I let be all types of life because they are expressions of human plurality and diversity. *Vive la difference!*'[12]

But this indifferent kind of tolerance is unable to explain the strong emotions that some religious practices arouse. The reason for this is that it underestimates how vulner-able we are when our values and identities are at stake, and completely negates the importance of their (public) recognition. That is why tolerance needs to be redefined in order to make sense again in order to deal with (the justification of) religious diversity. Following Ricoeur, from whose insights on tolerance I draw in this section, I propose to define tolerance as a virtue, in particular the virtue of asceticism in the exercise of power.[13] It can be summarized as follows: 'I disapprove of your manner of living, but I respect in it your liberty to live as you please and I recognize your right to manifest it publicly.'[14] It rests on the distinction between truth and justice: 'It is not in the name of truth as it appears to me [...] that I accept (and not simply endure) the other, but in the name of his equal right to mine to live his life as he seems fit.'[15] This kind of tolerance entitles individuals and collectivities to hold on to (the truth of) their religious values and practices, whether or not they are justified in the eyes of others, thereby doing justice to the current situation of heterogeneity of religious beliefs and practices. But it also requires people to abandon the asymmetry of power (the difference between acting and being acted upon), in favor of the reciprocal recognition of the right of others to exert their power of existing.

But this idea of tolerance as a virtue again raises the question of the distinction between justified and unjustified religious difference, although not on an epistemological, but on a practical level: how to deal with conflicting religious practices in a situation of cultural heterogeneity, especially when they appear to be unjustifiable, because harmful to others? In order to answer this question, we have to start from the experience of the intolerable, because it can be seen as the practical translation of unjustified religious difference. The reason that the intolerable is rejected as intolerable is that it does harm to other people. This explains why, paradoxically perhaps, the notion of the intolerable is essential for tolerance and, hence, also for dealing with conflicting religious practices in a peaceful way, especially in cases of harming others. The intolerable can be defined as 'what we would not want to tolerate, even though we could or even should.'[16] Of course, this notion is very problematic, because it implies that a limit is set to tolerance. But an unlimited tolerance cannot serve as the final answer to the question we are dealing with, because it eventually results in the erosion of tolerance as a virtue and its replacement by indifference, as well as in the negation of the no-harm principle.

So, my basic point is that the intolerable or the unjustified forms of religious diversity not only cannot be superseded, because the intolerable is a fundamental anthropological reality, but also should not disappear, because, paradoxically, it is a point of resistance against the erosion of tolerance. The intolerable is recognized by the passion of indignation it generates, and can be summarized as: 'We do not want to put up with all that!' But although the passion of indignation cannot serve as an unambiguous common ground for settling the discussion about justified versus unjustified (and unjustifiable) religious diversity, it nevertheless has an important heuristic function: it refers to our moral responsibility to oppose to all kinds of harms, which is based on the fundamental vulnerability of the human person. So, when reflecting on the passion of indignation that the experience of the intolerable causes in us, the question that crops up is: in the name of what are we indignant about the intolerable? Who can legitimately declare that certain expressions of the intolerable are not only unjustified but even unjustifiable? The answer to the first question refers to the moral principle of avoiding harm, and thus to the hidden sources of our culture and the values it stands for. It is always easier to point to what runs counter to fundamental human values than to positively define the sources of these values unambiguously, especially in times of a heterogeneity of cultures, religions, and values. Hence, the passion of indignation that the intolerable raises in us helps us to block moral indifference. The answer to the second question confronts us with the current situation of heterogeneity in a different way. Although some forms of harm can be defined quite unambiguously, especially in the case of material or physical harm, it is far more difficult when mental, emotional, cultural or environmental harm is at stake. These are far more context-dependent: while Aristotle justified slavery, this is nowadays considered as a gross violation of human dignity; whereas (almost unlimited) individual self-determination is enshrined in the constitution of most Western societies, other societies reject it as a complete negation of the vulnerable and social nature of the human person. However, the heterogeneity of the manifestations of harm is not identical with their incommensurability. Instead, this heterogeneity should make us aware of the fact that the 'who' of the declarations of the intolerable have to remain multiple.

When applying these thoughts about the intolerable to the question of religious difference, it is clear that the distinction between justified and unjustified religious difference remains of crucial importance, but rather on anthropological than on epistemological grounds. Furthermore, it is essential that the decision of what kinds of religious diversity are unjustified remains multiple. The legitimate claim that there are limits to religious diversity should not be considered as a stepping stone toward reconstituting an univocal moral or religious objectivity. It is only a small step from the indignation that the some intolerable practical consequences of religious diversity arouse in us to reinventing intolerance in order to limit the abuses of tolerance. Hence, in order to prevent this kind of intolerance from cropping up again behind the virtuous guise of unjustified religious diversity, a spirit of prudence is needed, which is the essence of practical wisdom. Practical wisdom means to content oneself with fragile compromises, and a careful weighing up of the pros and cons of the indignation about multiple expressions of the religiously intolerable or unjustifiable, without wanting to reach premature or forced conclusions of disputed questions, in particular of what needs to be qualified as unjustified rather than justified religious difference.

## Notes

1. Grube, Justified Religious Difference.
2. See Jonkers, "From Rational Doctrine to Christian Wisdom," 163–191.
3. Küng, *Global Responsibility*, xv.
4. For a good overview of this discussion see: Moyaert, *In Response to the Religious Other*, 69–92. In this and the following paragraphs, I regularly draw on her study.
5. Küng, *Yes to a Global Ethic*, 2.
6. Küng and Kuschel, *A Global Ethics*, 11–39.
7. Vroom, *Walking in a Widening World*, 271.
8. Moyaert, *In Response of the Religious Other*, 71.
9. See Rorty, "Science as Solidarity," 35–45.
10. At the end of his article Grube also mentions this as one of the political implications of justified religious difference.
11. I developed this question further in: Jonkers, "Can Freedom of Religion Replace the Virtue of Tolerance?" 73–84, and in Jonkers, "Do We just Have to Put Up With All That?"
12. Ricoeur, "The Erosion of Tolerance and the Resistance of the Intolerable," 191.
13. Ibid., 189.
14. Ibid., 191.
15. Ibid., 192.
16. Ibid., 197.

## Bibliography

Grube, D.-M. "Justified Religious Difference: A Constructive Approach to Religious Diversity." *International Journal of Philosophy and Theology* 76, no. 5 (2015): 419–427.

Jonkers, P. "Can Freedom of Religion Replace the Virtue of Tolerance?" Chap. 6 in *From Political Theory to Political Theology. Religious Challenges and the Prospects of Democracy*, edited by A. Singh and P. Losonczi, 73–84. London/New York: Continuum, 2010.

Jonkers, P. "From Rational Doctrine to Christian Wisdom. A Possible Response of the Church to Today's Seekers." Chap. 5 in *A Catholic Minority Church in a World of Seekers*, edited by S. Hellemans and P. Jonkers, 163–191. Washington, DC: Council for Research in Values and Philosophy, 2015.

Jonkers, P. "'Do We just Have to Put Up With All That?' Philosophical Reflections on Cultural Diversity and Tolerance." (Forthcoming).

Küng, H. *Global Responsibility: In Search of a New World Ethic*. New York: Crossroad, 1991.

Küng, H. *Yes to a Global Ethic*. London: SCM, 1996.

Küng, H., and K.-J. Kuschel. *A Global Ethics: The Declaration of the World's Religions*. London: SCM, 1993.

Moyaert, M. *In Response to the Religious Other. Ricoeur and the Fragility of Interreligious Encounters*. Lanham/Boulder/New York/London: Lexington Books, 2014.

Ricoeur, P. "The Erosion of Tolerance and the Resistance of the Intolerable." In *Between Intolerance and the Intolerable*, edited by P. Ricoeur, 189–201. Oxford: Berghahn, 1996.

Rorty, R. "Science as Solidarity." In *Objectivity, Relativism, and Truth*, edited by R. Rorty, 35–45. Cambridge: Cambridge University Press, 1990.

Vroom, H. M. *Walking in a Widening World: Understanding Religious Diversity*. Amsterdam: VU University Press, 2013.

# A theological alternative to Grube's notion of 'justified religious difference'

Luco J. van den Brom

Grube proposes a framework for respectful dealing with different religions: 'justified religious difference. The author comments on the epistemic setting of Grube's thesis. It testifies a cognitive approach to religious faith by handling religious faith and epistemic belief as analogous argument. His criticism of the pluralist approach is not very convincing. This framework is too abstract for an interreligious dialogue. The author proposes a concept of religious faith within a web of practices, liturgical rituals. A concrete interreligious dialogue can enrich the Christian faith in its practical styling.

Modern Western societies show a plurality of activities of different religious traditions. In the first part of the twentieth century, Europe was called a Christian continent and other religions used to belong to other continents. In contrast, the twenty-first-century street scene of most European big cities is characterized by the presence of different faiths. These faiths are often practiced one next to another. Interestingly, in spite of the differences in their practices, adherents of these religions recognize each other's practices as religious time and again. This is a striking phenomenon because we cannot easily define what religion is. Not only do we call, e.g. Judaism, Christianity, Islam or Hinduism religions, but also Buddhism, Taoism, Confucianism and Sikhism.

However, upon comparing religions, it is difficult to find some common elements as essentially defining characteristics which we might consider as the common denominator of 'all' religions. That is, we can observe that some of these specific religions share many characteristics but differ in any concrete instance of a comparison. Therefore, we should talk about religions in Wittgensteinian terminology of 'family resemblances': each religion shares some characteristics with any other religion, but there are no characteristics shared by *all*. In other words, we cannot define 'religion' as this or that sort of thing in order to distinguish between true and false religion.[1] In his inaugural lecture, Professor Dirk-Martin Grube proposes a framework for dealing with different religions: he calls this framework 'justified religious difference' which 'allows for tolerance and respect for other religions than the home religion' (419). This framework is based on the non-traditional epistemological perspective with which Grube agrees. Non-traditional epistemology is based upon the insight that we may call someone's belief of $p$ a case of knowing $p$ if her belief of $p$ originates in reliable cognitive procedures given her circumstances. According to Grube, she is *justified* in holding the belief that $p$ if she has carefully collected the available evidence of the belief for $p$.

Therefore, whether someone is justified to hold the belief that *p* depends on the epistemological circumstances and perspectives that that person happens to be in. According to Grube, the most important implication is that different epistemological perspectives 'allow to justify different but *equally* legitimate beliefs ... on the same issue' (423; emphasis added). Thus, we may expect a plurality of different legitimate beliefs which allows us to acknowledge legitimate 'otherness' in epistemological perspectives. Because of this insight, Grube attacks biased explanations which do not acknowledge the possibility of genuine 'otherness' as being justifiably different. His framework for dealing with different *religious* viewpoints is based on the application of the same epistemological insight in a religious context, so that different religious perspectives may allow the justification of holding different legitimate *religious beliefs*. 'As little as we have to condemn all deviant beliefs as being false – if we acknowledge justified difference, we do not have to condemn all deviant religious beliefs as being false – if we acknowledge justified difference in religion' (424). Grube is of the opinion that many pluralist approaches to religious diversity attempt to minimize the differences between the divergent religions. With that purpose in view, pluralists such as John Hick postulate a unity between or beyond the different religions: Hick's proposal is to consider the major world religions as related to a transcendent '*Real an sich*', as 'an ultimate divine Reality' which lies behind or beyond all the varied visions of it. If within the perspective of one's own religious tradition all forms of religious experience can be seen in one way or another as a cognitive response to a divine reality, it is rationally justified to have the same attitude towards religious experiences of other traditions, according to Hick.[2] In a sense we may agree with Grube that Hick is minimizing and ignoring the characteristic differences between the divergent religions: as noumenon the '*Real an sich*' is unknowable and indescribable. This notion is basic for Hick's model in order to be all-encompassing for all religions by transcending the contradictory claims of divergent religions: the '*Real an sich*' functions as a religious umbrella concept.

Hick's 'pluralistic hypothesis' presents a *monotypic* form of religious reductionism because at the end of the day all major religions relate to the same '*Real*'. However, a 'pluralist hypothesis' tries to justify all sorts of religious perspectives as equally valid. To justify a religious perspective, we need a broader context that supplies us with criteria to evaluate that perspective. How to justify Hick's all-encompassing 'pluralist hypothesis' as a religious perspective? We cannot justify it in its *own* terms, because then it is justified by definition. A pluralist paradigm seems to transcend its own specific perspective by providing a new framework that may be the context of all contexts. Such a God's Eye point of view as a View From Nowhere is not available for human observers and therefore meaningless.[3]

Grube's own critique goes one step further and concerns a presupposition which pluralists may share, that is the principle of *bivalence*. This principle states that declarative statements have one and not more than one truth value: they are *either* true *or* false. In the present context of how to deal with religious diversity, this principle causes problems in the interreligious dialogue. It implies that if position A is true and position B differs from A, B *must* be false: given a bivalent logic, there is no choice. However, this seems a problematic presentation of bivalent logic? Position B can only deny position A either if B is equivalent to non-A or if B implies non-A. This principle of bivalence implies an *equation between difference and falsity*, according to Grube. The consequence of this putative presupposition is devastating in the interreligious dialogue: if interlocutors discover genuine differences between their religions, they *have to* consider each other's religion to be false, even though pluralists would prefer otherwise. Therefore pluralists 'are driven ... to downplay difference since difference is taken to equal falsity' (421) and to stress the similarities between religions. However, Grube does not provide any arguments in support of this putative pluralist presupposition of the principle of *bivalence*. Instead, he merely says: 'I suspect that many pluralist ... attempts presuppose this equation' (421).

'Being suspicious' is not a logical but psychological argument! It tells about Grube's opinion but nothing about the special logic presupposed by the pluralist model of religion such as that defended by John Hick, say. Hick rejects both a sceptical and an exclusivist view on religious experience and proposes a third possibility, namely that the great faiths constitute different ways of experiencing an ultimate divine Reality. He illustrates the fruitfulness of his proposal by means of several examples which can be dealt with by his pluralistic hypothesis. Hick's hypothesis is an ontological claim, whereas Grube rejects the putative logic of the pluralists – i.e. the two-value or bivalent logic – by agreeing with Joseph Margolis's proposal to use a multi-valued logic. And then – to my amazement – he *changes the subject* and leaves the topic of logic and ontology and continues to speak on the *epistemological* notion of justification. Such an epistemological starting point in the interreligious dialogue implies that the interlocutors are open to religious otherness and will listen to deviant religious insights given the possibility that they can be justified given the epistemic circumstances of the believers who hold them. So far so good.

Grube's proposal of a framework for dealing with religious diversity presupposes that interlocutors have reflected upon what justifies them in holding their beliefs in their *epistemic* circumstances. The basic assumption of 'justified religious difference' is Grube's conviction that we can handle 'religious belief' and 'epistemic belief' in an analogous way. We can argue in support of our epistemic belief that, e.g., the moon is spherical and not flat by means of rational interpretations of our observations, given our epistemic circumstances. And in an analogous way, it is possible to argue that religious beliefs might be reasonable, given our religious epistemic circumstances – although not reasonable for everybody perhaps. Here, there is at least a conceptual difficulty, however. Religious belief and epistemic belief are not simply equivalent although we use the same sign 'belief'. Epistemic belief involves knowledge of propositions on how to do something ('practical knowledge') or on what to expect sometime somewhere ('knowledge by description'). However, it is also meaningful to say 'I know her in person'. This statement does not mean that I can reproduce a complete set of statements about this person but that I am familiar with this person. Analytic philosophers call this kind of knowledge 'knowledge by acquaintance'.

Religious belief is comparable to such 'knowledge by acquaintance', namely that is on the basis of some personal confrontation with specific religious practices. The historian of theology Robert Wilken writes about the conversion of Justin Martyr. He observes that, according to Justin, the message of Christ enters the life of a person on two levels: the moral and the intellectual level. 'The knowledge of God has to do with how one lives, with acting on convictions that are not mere premises but realities learned from *other* persons and tested by experience.'[4] This reminds me of the notion of Polanyi's 'personal knowledge': 'God is a commitment involved in our rites and myths. Through our integrative, imaginative efforts, we see him as the focal point that fuses into meaning all the incompatibles involved in the practice of religion.'[5] One implication of Wilken's remark concerns the meaning of religious concepts and statements: the meaning of these basic religious elements and utterances can be learned from how believers live. *They* are the peers. Both religious rituals and moral behaviour inform us about what *this* faith is doing and what it means for the community of believers. However, Grube considers religious differences within an epistemological perspective by asking how believers could justify and legitimate their beliefs. It seems he is treating religious beliefs and statements like knowledge claims. In that light he suggests that 'different epistemological contexts ... allow to justify different but equally legitimate beliefs' (423). And he goes even a step further: 'Once I have realized that you are *justified* in believing the religious beliefs you hold, there is no need to explain them' (425). I was amazed to hear that Grube leaves out the clause 'given *your* epistemic circumstances'. This clause seems crucial to me in Grube's argumentation on why to respect *you* in your religious otherness as my interlocutor, because I can agree that you are justified to hold your beliefs *given these special* circumstances.

In the last paragraph, Grube indicates that we need criteria which allow us to distinguish between justified and *un*justified religious differences. He is aware that he neglected the development of the criteria for making such a distinction which is very important to start an interreligious dialogue by understanding and making sense of each other's belief. Grube hopes to be able to take up this issue in the future! I will suggest a criterion, if I may. Imagine that religious beliefs and statements are never isolated knowledge claims but they are always part of a more encompassing way of life including particular religious rituals, ceremonies and other practices. Such practices also include a tradition of debate on how to cope with questions of life in a changing world and on the sense in which re-adjudgements of religious statements are possible and needed to maintain the viability of a faith. This means that talking about religion in general and religious diversity in broad and abstract terms neglects the actual network which individual religious rituals, practices or beliefs are part of. An interreligious dialogue is a conversation between adherents of particular religions, e.g. between Hindus and Muslims, between Jews and Christians, between Sikhs and Buddhists, etc. Nevertheless, even though Grube is focused solely on philosophical reasons for respecting other religions, he tries to make a strong case for his theoretical framework ('justified religious difference') in a sympathetic way. He avoids arguing from his own Christian commitment, but argues that he *knows* that others can be justified to hold their deviant beliefs. However, would he call *this* knowledge 'justified true belief' too? Such a premise would leave open the possibility that others could be *not* justified to hold deviant beliefs. Therefore I am confused by the remark in the last paragraph that there are religious differences which are *un*-justified. When would you be sure that your interlocutor is *not* justified to hold his deviant beliefs?

Grube creates this problem himself by generalizing his conversation about religious diversity, whereas the justification of a deviant epistemological perspective would only make sense in the case of a concrete particular perspective, i.e. the case of the perspective from within a particular faith. In that case, it is a real possibility that this specific religious perspective is justifiable. Simultaneously there is the real possibility that this perspective is not justifiable! I could ignore this last possibility but in that case would the concept of 'justified true beliefs' still enable me to participate in an interreligious dialogue as a sincere interlocutor who is capable 'to grasp the other's authentic being'? Being a Christian and a theologian reflecting upon the Christian way of life I can raise the question why God the Father confronts me/us with Muslims and Hindus. What would God want to make unequivocally clear to these specific Christians about their religious perspective through people who hold their clearly deviant beliefs, and celebrate their clearly deviant ceremonies and rituals? I know these questions are typically theological but they are philosophically justifiable by stressing the notion of 'family resemblances' between empirical religions: in such interactions, Christianity may receive new impulses which can enrich Christian faith, liturgy, practices, spirituality, etc. Interreligious dialogue can be revealing for Christians!

## Acknowledgement

I thank the anonymous referees for their constructive remarks.

## Notes

1. See van den Brom, "God, Gödel and Trinity," 56–76, esp. 59.
2. Hick, *An Interpretation of Religion*, 235–238.
3. van den Brom, "God, Gödel and Trinity," 70–73.
4. Wilken, *The Spirit of Early Christian Thought*, 7; my italics.
5. Polanyi and Prosch, *Meaning*, 156.

## Bibliography

Grube, D.-M. "Justified Religious Difference. A Constructive Approach to Religious Diversity." *International Journal of Philosophy and Theology* 76, no. 5 (2015): 419–427.

Hick, J. *An Interpretation of Religion: Human Responses to the Transcendent*, 235–238. Basingstoke: Macmillan Press, 1989.

Polanyi, M., and H. Prosch. *Meaning*. Chicago: Chicago University Press, 1975.

van den Brom, L. J. "God, Gödel and Trinity: A Contribution to the Theology of Religions." In *Christian Faith and Philosophical Theology*, Ed. G. van den Brink, L. J. van den Brom, and M. Sarot, 56–76. Kampen: Kok Pharos Publishing House, 1992.

Wilken, R. L. *The Spirit of Early Christian Thought: Seeking the Face of God*. New Haven: Yale University Press, 2003.

# CONCLUDING REMARKS

## Reply to the respondents to 'Justified religious difference. A constructive approach to religious diversity'

Dirk-Martin Grube

In this reply, I take up the challenges the five respondents raised. In particular, I deal with the issues of truth, bivalence (respectively *tertium non datur*), tolerance, and justification.

By way of their *genre*, inaugural lectures are condensed and rather broad since they are addressed to a mixed audience. The following theses develop and defend my thoughts on the 'justified religious difference' paradigm (if it is one) in greater depth. To that end, I will take up and elaborate on the issues the respondents have raised.

Given the background of the respondents, it is not surprising that they raise primarily epistemological issues, such as bivalence, truth, and justification (tolerance being the exception). Those issues are important for my account and I delve into them in my inaugural lecture at length. Yet, I would like to point out here that they are primarily important only for the 'justified difference' part of the 'justified religious difference'-paradigm. That is, they are important as a basis or *foundation* of the paradigm, not so much for a further elaboration of the paradigm as such.

The paradigm as such, however, is more comprehensive and implies a number of different aspects regarding the interaction between different religions. At some of them I have hinted in my inaugural lecture, viz.

- a particular way to deal with the religious Other (which takes her Otherness seriously),
- a particular, possibly reconstructed, way to frame the interreligious dialogue (without bivalent presuppositions or, as I call them below, without exclusivist kinds of competitions),
- a particular, possibly 'novel' way to understand the function of the activity of arguing in the context of this dialogue,
- and last but not least, it implies moral and political consequences (I hint at some of them when discussing Jonkers' account of tolerance below, section 8).

These and related issues make up the paradigm of 'justified religious difference'. Yet, although I hope to be able to take them up in the future, I will not discuss them in depth in this reply since none of the respondents has raised them extensively. Thus, the following considerations focus predominantly on the foundation of this paradigm, viz. on a particular *theory of alterity* which I call *justified difference*.

Yet, although impacting only the foundation, the epistemological issues the respondents have raised are nevertheless of crucial importance. They provide the building blocks for a (hopefully) sound theory of alterity. Such a theory, i.e. a coherent and theoretically well thought-through way to deal with Otherness, is highly urgent in our current context: In Europe and elsewhere, people holding different, often seriously different, religious, cultural, and related beliefs live side by side in the same public space. The challenges this causes are intensified by the fact that large numbers of refugees from mostly Islamic countries and with foreign cultural and intellectual backgrounds seek asylum in some European countries. Thus, it is highly urgent to reflect on the issue of (religious) alterity in a serious fashion, in a philosophically and politically responsible fashion. I hope to contribute to this discussion with the following considerations.

As is common in philosophical discussions, the respondents focus predominantly on the issues they disagree with. In this reply, I will proceed in a similar fashion, viz. by focusing on those issues raised by the respondents with which I disagree.

Yet, although I will not dwell on the agreements in the following, I would like to mention in passing that the fact that all respondents (with the possible exception of *van den Brom[1]*) agree with my rejection of religious pluralism is, at least, worth mentioning. The pluralist paradigm, thus the search for common ground between the religions, has dominated the interreligious dialogue for quite some time and is still alive in many of its quarters. If the respondents agree with my suggestion that Hick and others do *not* provide the solution to the issue at stake, we have reached an agreement which is, at least, worth a mention.

These concluding remarks are structured as follows: In the remainder of this section, I will summarize the gist of the argument of my inaugural lecture (the italicized numbers point to the sections in which the issue at stake is elaborated further). Furthermore, in sections 1 and 2, I provide some basic clues as to what I mean by *truth*, in sections 3 to 6, I take up the issue of *bivalence*, in sections 7 to 8, that of *tolerance*, and in sections 9 to 11, that of *justification*.

The argument in my inaugural lecture can be summarized as follows:

- If we wish to have a constructive (i.e. non-exclusivist) and positive (e.g. respectful, acknowledging,[2] etc.) attitude towards other religions than the home-religion, reducing the differences between the deviant religions in the way religious pluralists such as Hick do will not work.
- Rather, we need an alternative account that allows us to take religious differences seriously, i.e. allows us to acknowledge religious Otherness without reducing it.
- In order to achieve this, we need to break through the equation of difference with falsity. That is, that which is different must not automatically be considered to be false.
- For the purposes of breaking through this equation, we must question the logical principles of bivalence/*tertium non datur*. In order to do so, we should distinguish between different realms of inquiry, viz. those in which those principles are applicable and those in which they are not. The latter are realms in which the objects are of such a sort that treating them under bivalent parameters would fail to do justice to them. An example is Margolis's world of culture (e.g. the arts; see above, my inaugural lecture). In my view, many religious beliefs belong into this category as well (see *sections 3–5*).

- There are different ways how to proceed responsibly in those realms in which bivalence is not applicable: Examples are to rely on *non*-bivalent conceptions of truth (such as a many-valued logic), to substitute truth by the notion of 'entitlement', or to substitute it by 'justification'.

- I choose the latter way for the reasons mentioned below (see section 9). One of them is that the notion of justification has been discussed intensively in epistemology. The upshot of this discussion is (in my view) that justification is context-dependent in a way in which truth is not. As a consequence, justification can be pluralized in a way in which truth cannot: Agents in different contexts, in different epistemic (and probably also non-epistemic) circumstances, can be justified to hold different beliefs on the same issue (see *sections 9–10*).

- This pluralization of justification is the basis upon which 'justified difference' rests: My intuition – admittedly not more than alluded to in the inaugural lecture – is that it makes a significant difference whether we disagree with a (set of) beliefs on the grounds that they are straightforwardly false or on grounds short of truth-geared ones. The latter, disagreeing with deviant beliefs on grounds short of truth-considerations proper, seems to me to be a promising basis for a theory of alterity worth its name, i.e. a theory which allows to respect the Other in her Otherness (see *section 11*).

- In my inaugural lecture, I suggest that our attitude towards other religions should be reconstructed along the lines of this theory of alterity: We disagree with them indeed, yet, not on the grounds that they are straightforwardly false. Once we acknowledge that, we will approach those other religions and their members in a different, more positive, way than as if we assume that the beliefs those religions imply are false. This is the *core of the justified religious difference-paradigm*.

## Truth

### *1. The notion of truth*

Since the notion of truth plays a crucial role in my argument as well as in the responses, I will first specify what I mean by 'truth'.

The notion of truth I have in mind is a *semantic* one in the broad sense of the term. By 'semantic', I mean that our words, terms, thoughts, consciousness, *intellectus*… relate to the world, things, *rei*, or whatever else has been suggested in the philosophical tradition. By labeling this notion 'semantic' in the *broad* sense of the term, I wish to stay clear of the classical philosophical discussions on how this relationship is to be characterized precisely, whether it is one of mirroring, reflecting, *adequatio*, or something else along those lines.

In other words, I suggest a broad characterization of truth without committing myself to any of the classical theories of truth as suggested by Thomas von Aquino, German idealism, the early Wittgenstein or whoever else comes to mind. Nor do I wish to defend here (Quinean-inspired) holist forms of realism that I have defended elsewhere. My point here is simply to insist that truth has the function to portray reality, in whichever way 'portray' and 'reality' are to be understood precisely.

Classifying truth as a semantic notion is a sort of *meta*-characterization and not a definition of it. Obviously, it has some resemblances with a correspondence theory of truth. Yet, I do not wish to commit myself here to such a theory nor to the problems inherent in it (such as the issue whether 'correspondence' functions not only as a definition but also as a criterion for truth). Rather, I wish to stay clear of all attempts to *define* truth in the strict sense of the word. All I wish to insist on is that whatever definition of truth is suggested has to meet this semantic character.

I take this semantic character to be the most important feature of any (meta-) characterization of truth. Frankly, I think that a semantic notion of truth has an anthropological basis: We need to search for (semantic) truth if we wish to be faithful to what characterizes us as human beings. By this I do not (only) mean some kind of Darwinist rationale, say, that we need to know what reality is like in order to survive. Rather, I mean that our search for (semantic) truth has to do with our Intentional, lingual,[3] conscious, etc. nature. Thus, one of the most important reasons why we search for semantic truth is simply that we are the kinds of beings that we are.

Yet, I realize that this may sound absurd in an age in which anthropology is either neglected from the philosophical side or, else, has become the playing field for an unrestrained (and often un-reflected) materialism. It may thus be wise to provide a less strenuous rationale for why the search for truth is indispensable. Here is one: Truth in the semantic sense specified lies at the bottom of many practices we employ, among them those which are most dear to us. Without presupposing it, those practices would not make much sense.

An example is the practice of providing arguments. Without presupposing a semantic notion of truth, this practice would not be what it is. For example, without presupposing it right now, I would do something else than what I am doing at this moment. I would, e.g. be entertaining, trying to trick the reader, or whatever rather than *arguing* for the indispensability of semantic truth. My point is thus that semantic truth is something like a *transcendental presupposition for many of the practices we* are engaged in, among them many which we value highly. If we wish to make sense of those practices, we have to presuppose truth in the semantic sense.

Since I regard the semantic sense of truth to be as indispensable as I have just sketched, I have little sympathy with postmodernists and others who trivialize or ridicule truth in this sense (see the criticism of Rorty in my inaugural lecture): They betray this 'transcendental' character of truth, let alone its anthropological foundation. If our truth-telling would be nothing more than 'edifying' in Rorty's sense, i.e. 'exciting',[4] than many of our practices would not be any longer what they are and we would probably fail to do justice to our human nature.

Yet, if we consider (semantic) truth to be a transcendental presupposition for important practices we are engaged in or even grounded in anthropology – as I suggest – it follows that we have an *obligation to maximize it*. As a corollary, we have an obligation to *minimize falsity*. If we would fail to maximize truth and minimize falsity, we would betray our human nature or, at least, the presuppositions upon which many of our practices rest upon. If we would fail to do so, we would, e.g. be increasingly incapable of providing the (transcendental) rationale for practices such as that of arguing.

Furthermore, given the semantic character of truth, it follows that *truth is one*. At least, under the ontological assumption that reality is one rather than many,[5] we have to assume that truth is one, at least, ideally. This is a straightforward corollary of its semantic character: If truth's function is to portray reality and reality is one, truth must ideally be one rather than many.

Yet, it is important to keep this idealization in mind: *Ideally*, truth is one. Yet, this does not mean that we are in all cases capable of deciding what truth value to apply in a given case. Put differently: We are not always capable of distributing the bipolar pair of truth values, 'true/false', over pertinent statements. Whether or not we are depends, among others, on the domain of inquiry in question. For example, Margolis' 'world of culture' (see above) is a domain in which this is not (always) possible.

Furthermore, I insist on the indispensability of the semantic character of the quest for truth, *not* on truth as such. That is, given the beings we are and the presupposition of practices as that of arguing, we cannot fail to attempt portraying reality. Yet, by what means we do is open to discussion. In cases in which bivalent truth is not available, we should resort to other means, such as non-bivalent notions of truth or notions such as entitlement or justification. Both of the latter are pragmatic rather than semantic notions – i.e. they refer to the characteristics of people holding beliefs rather than characteristics of the beliefs themselves. Yet, they serve, ultimately, semantic purposes. That is, entitlement and justification (in the epistemic sense) are geared towards truth.[6]

## 2. Truth and religious beliefs (criticizing van Woudenberg)

*Van Woudenberg* insists that religious beliefs imply truth claims. He claims that it is an 'empirical fact' that most religious people 'fully accept' bivalence. They hold their own religious beliefs to be true and competing ones to be false (see above).

I can conceive of two ways to understand this claim: First, literally as an empirical claim or, second, as a normative claim camouflaged in descriptive terms. If it is to be understood in the first sense, I am not sure what follows from it. I admit that many religious people do use terms such as 'truth'. But do they really mean it in the philosophical, strictly bivalent sense that is at stake here?

But even if they would, this would not provide an overriding reason why we should follow their use of terminology. It may well be legitimate to *reconstruct* their use of the notion of truth. Reconstructing 'ordinary' religious believers word usage is nothing uncommon and philosophers of religion are used to it. In itself, this is not illegitimate. It is as little illegitimate as it is for the philosopher of science to reconstruct 'ordinary' beliefs about causality (e.g. in terms of statistical probabilities).[7]

Yet, my suspicion is that van Woudenberg has the second, normative use in mind: Rather than providing a description of how the majority of believers *does* believe he means to suggest that they *should* believe in truth in the way he indicates.[8]

But what would it imply to suggest that religious beliefs should be subjected to bivalent treatment? It would imply to treat them analogously to the way *statements* in the strict sense of the term (see below) are treated. Yet, if they were statements, the believer would be under an obligation to demonstrate their truth.

If this is what he means, van Woudenberg puts a heavy burden on the shoulders of the believer. If so, he owes us an explanation how the believer is supposed to carry this heavy burden. Is she supposed to supply sufficient evidence for the truth of her beliefs? If so, how, precisely? An issue important in this regard is, e.g. how much evidence is 'sufficient' to be rationally entitled to hold one's religious beliefs: Will it do if the believer supplies evidence to the effect that the probability that her beliefs are true is higher than 50%? Or is more required?

Or does van Woudenberg expect the believer to demonstrate the truth of her religious beliefs along *rationalist* rather than empiricist lines? If so, how should she proceed precisely? Should she endorse one of the traditional arguments for the existence of God? If so, which argument does van Woudenberg consider to be successful?[9]

If we follow van Woudenberg's suggestion that religious believers should consider their beliefs to be true, a line of argument he endorses elsewhere will *not* do in this case. I mean the line suggested by (some) Reformed Epistemologists, viz. that believers are 'entitled' (in Woltertorff's sense; see section 9) to their beliefs or that no serious arguments speak against holding them (in Alvin Plantinga's sense[10]). This line of argument comes close to the spirit in which *I* distinguish truth from justification and I endorse the principle underlying it.[11] But it will not do for van Woudenberg's current purposes. If I understand him correctly, he wishes to go beyond suggesting that believers are entitled to hold their religious beliefs. Rather, he suggests that believers should hold them to be *true*.

Let me add a personal remark at this point: Having studied the matter for some thirty plus years, I still do not know how to demonstrate the truth of my Christian beliefs. Rather than desperately trying to demonstrate their truth I am content to know that I have *reasons* to be justified to hold them (one of them being the poverty of atheism; see below). I am afraid that aspiring more, viz. to squeeze religious beliefs into the Procrustes-bed of the 'truth/falsity' alternative plays only into the cards of the despisers of religion.

Let me furthermore alert you to the fact that the concept of bivalent truth at stake here is a *philosophical* construct and not necessarily a religious one. Looking at my own, Christian, religion the Hebrew equivalent of truth, *ämät*, has different connotations than a bivalent conception of truth has: *Ämät* points to a realm of being which is dominated by God's faithfulness and reliability in spite of the appearance to the opposite. The most important aspect of 'truth' in this sense is to accord from the human side with this realm by *trusting* God's faithfulness.[12]

In short, I disagree with van Woudenberg that religious people should consider their beliefs to be true in the bivalent sense of the word. At least, given the specifications of truth as provided above, they should not (obviously, they are free to consider their beliefs to be true in another sense of the word). I cannot speak for other religions but insist that Christians should not. Rather, Christians should insist that the proper epistemic status for their beliefs is something in the neighborhood of 'I *hope* that my Christian beliefs are true'.

To be sure, this hope is not without reasons. One of them is the intellectual poverty of (much of) atheism. At least, my own reasons for hoping that my Christian beliefs are true are fed to a good extent by the knowledge that much of atheism is based upon intellectually questionable strategies. Among those questionable strategies are claiming unearned (cognitive, discursive, or related) privileges,[13] claiming an unearned default status for atheism,[14] over-interpreting the argument that the religious belief-generating mechanisms are unreliable,[15] over-interpreting the criticism that *some* religious beliefs are incoherent,[16] and metaphysical speculation.[17]

My argument is *not* that the demise of atheism demonstrates convincingly the plausibility of theism. This would be nothing but to turn tables and make use of the kind of questionable argumentative strategies (some) atheists use. Yet, I suggest that atheism's weakness is *one of a variety of reasons* why I think to be justified to hold the Christian beliefs I hold.[18]

## Bivalence

### 3. *Margolis's criticism of bivalence*

Those respondents who have an affinity with the analytic tradition of philosophy have jumped (predictably) on the way I deal with bivalence: Brümmer and van Woudenberg strongly reject my criticism of it, Pihlström, coming more from a pragmatist rather than strictly analytic background, is more moderate by rejecting only some aspects of this criticism.

Before commenting on the respondents' remarks, however, let me first extend my thanks to Brümmer and van Woudenberg for the specifications they made concerning bivalence (that it applies only if genuine statements are at stake which are on the same issue and contradict each other, etc.). I accept (almost) all of them.

In particular, I acknowledge Brümmer's point that the law of excluded middle, *tertium non datur*, is to be distinguished from bivalence: There exist semantics[19] which satisfy this law but are not bivalent. My real issue lies as much with *tertium non datur* as with bivalence. Therefore, I will use the term 'bivalence/*tertium non datur*' in the following. And 'bivalent terminology' is shorthand for 'bivalence *and tertium non datur*' in the following.

I acknowledge also that my treatment of bivalence in the inaugural lecture is extremely condensed. As I made clear in the summary of my argument at the beginning of this feedback, I mean by 'abrogating bivalence' something like 'abrogating the principled insistence on bivalence' (respectively 'bivalence/*tertium non datur*'). This has to do with the background I presuppose, viz. the discussion on bivalence/*tertium non datur* in philosophy. I summarize the issues of this discussion that are relevant for my current purposes in the following.

In some quarters of the Anglo-American philosophy, bivalence/*tertium non datur* have been discussed extensively in the last four decades or so. I think particularly of Michael Dummett who had criticized bivalence but exempted *tertium non datur* from this criticism. He suggested that, once the question of decidability is answered positively, for no statement 'can we ever rule out both the possibility of its being true and that of its being false...'[20]

Margolis has taken up Dummett on the issue of decidability. Margolis argues that telling us that something is not undecidable as a matter of principle is not telling us very much. Unless decidability is indexicalized, i.e. unless time constraints are provided as to *when* something will be decided, promising us that it *can* be decided is an empty promise. Unless we are told when the issue of the truth of statements can be decided – by 'us' now, by future generations, by supercomputers in the year 3000? – promising us that they can does not get us very far.[21]

In a later stage of his career, roughly, from the 1990s onwards, Margolis uses the criticism of bivalence as a spring board for more general considerations: He argues now that, in certain domains of inquiry, bivalence should be abrogated. His prime example are the arts. He suggests that contradictory statements, say, interpretations of the Potato-Eater from a Marxist and a Freudian view, should be tolerated simultaneously.

The general point he now emphasizes is that reflections about truth cannot be fixed in abstraction from the domain of inquiry at stake. He argues that 'the choice of truth values...assigned...to any sector of inquiry is a function...of what we take the nature of the domain in question'[22] to be. In other words, whether we think that the principle of bivalence/*tertium non datur* is applicable or not *depends on the nature of the objects* at stake. In some domains of inquiry, the objects are of such a nature that it is applicable, in others such that it is not.

I subscribe to Margolis's criticism of bivalence.[23] But different from what *van Woudenberg* and *Brümmer* think, I do *not* mean to suggest that contradictory beliefs can both be *true*. Rather, I suggest that, in certain domains of inquiry, the objects are of such a nature that the principle of bivalence does not apply. In those domains, we can be justified to hold deviating[24] beliefs. That is, in cases in which the issue of truth cannot be fixed in a determinate sense, it is conceivable that deviating views are justified.

The focus of my criticism is thus the *universal pretensions* implied in the principles of bivalence and *tertium non datur*. I mean the pretension that they are *laws of logic*, thus universally valid, laws without which we cannot think or cannot think rationally.

I wish to raise our consciousness for the difference between a principle being truly a law of logic, thus, a precondition for rational thinking, and a principle being nothing more than a particular way of thinking, however desirable, prudent, etc. it may be. Take as an example the *principium rationis sufficientis*, i.e. the maxim that we always have to provide sufficient reasons for our arguments. In older books on logic still considered to be a logical axiom, closer scrutiny has revealed that it is nothing but a particular way of thinking.[25]

My point here is not so much to criticize this principle as such but to criticize the universal pretensions implied in the claim that it is a law of logic. It sails under the flag of universal validity, of being a precondition for rational thinking, whereas it is nothing but a partisan, contingent, time-bound way of thinking.

Worse, in some cases, universal validity claims are abused to smuggle in particular ideologies without admitting it openly. This can be exemplified by (post-)Russellian analyses of reference: In response to the so-called problem of the 'truth value gaps', viz. that statements on fictional entities possess neither the truth value 'true' nor 'false', Russell introduced an analysis of reference which makes the act of successful referring dependent upon the existence of the object of reference.[26] Apart from the fact that this maneuver misconstrues reference – after all, we *can* successfully refer to, say, Gandalf the Grey – it is a convenient way to smuggle into the theory of reference a (British[27]) empiricist ideology.

Again, my primary issue here is not to reject empiricism but to point out the manipulative character of Russell's and related maneuvers: They come under the guise of providing a theory of reference, neutral as theories of this sort are supposed to be. But what they do is to use this supposedly neutral theory for the purposes of selling their favorite doctrine, viz. empiricism. My criticism pertains to 'salesmen-tricks' of this sort.

The lesson to be learnt from those examples is that we should be highly suspicious of all supposedly neutral claims with universal pretensions.[28] All too often they are abused to smuggle in this or that ideology. I thus suggest that we should analyze them very critically and ask in every instance whether they are *truly* universal or nothing but ways to 'sell' this or that ideology under the flag of universal claims.

Thus, we should be suspicious of bivalence/*tertium non datur* as well if they come with universal pretensions. In particular, I have two concerns with them, an ontological and an epistemological one: My *ontological* concern is that a principled insistence on them presupposes that the world is such that it can be sliced up neatly into 'true' and 'false' facts. My *epistemological* concern is that they presuppose a cognitive ideal according to which we humans are always capable of deciding properly which statements on this world are true and which are false.

Yet, the ontological presupposition is based in my view on a fictional purism that fails to notice the world's messy, untidy character. And the epistemological presupposition is based upon a *Prometheian* ideal that seriously overestimates human cognitive capabilities. Last but not least, I reject cognitive *Prometheism* for *theological* reasons since I think it fails to appreciate the full extent of the cognitive consequences the 'fallen' status of humankind has.

## 4. (Criticizing) Pihlström, Brümmer, and van Woudenberg on bivalence

Yet, I will not delve into the reasons for being suspicious of a principled insistence on bivalence/*tertium non datur* any further here.[29] Rather, I wish to reflect on how Pihlström's, Brümmer's, and van Woudenberg's criticism of my position fare in light of the above clarifications on what I mean by bivalence/*tertium non datur*.

*Pihlström* criticizes my position by suggesting that I go too far. He agrees with the point that a 'plurality of different beliefs could be legitimate (justified)' but thinks that this point can be had without abrogating the principle of bivalence. He thinks that a general fallibilism will do according to which we acknowledge that our beliefs, including our religious beliefs, could be false. Regarding bivalence, he proposes that we 'only need to pay attention to where exactly that principle is relevant' (see above).

I fully concur with Pihlström's last point. This is exactly what I (following Margolis) mean by suggesting that bivalence should be abrogated only in certain domains of inquiry, not *tout court*. As indicated above, my point is only to reject the universal pretensions that come with bivalence.

Yet, I am more skeptical about Pihlström's first point: How are we supposed to acknowledge a legitimate plurality of different beliefs *within* bivalent parameters? I cannot help but thinking that bivalence inevitably entails an exclusivist competition between beliefs (see section 5, for a fuller treatment of the relationship between bivalence and exclusivist competitions). It entails that only the belief A *or* B (whereby 'or' is understood in the logical, i.e. exclusivist sense) can be true, not that both can. Certainly, the fallibilism Philström suggests offers no solace at this point. Acknowledging that my beliefs could be false does not relativize the exclusivist 'or'. It leads only to the suggestion that if my belief A is false your belief B is true. Yet, my point is not to substitute A with B but to provide a framework within which *both* A *and* B can be legitimate or justified.

If I understand *Brümmer* correctly, he subscribes to the view that *tertium non datur* or excluded middle are universally valid. He suggests that it is an 'essential requirement for the possibility of making any statement at all, or more generally, for the success of any legitimate speech act' (see above).

I am not sure whether Brümmer means the same thing by *tertium non datur* as I do. But if so, I strongly disagree. Let me explain this with the help of an example I will explain more extensively below. In my view, uttering

> Given (my knowledge of) the current state of the research on the issue, I am incapable of distributing the bipolar pair of truth values over the statement 'the exhaustion of carbon dioxides is the most important cause of the current climate-changes'

seems to me to be a perfectly legitimate speech act.

Under some definitions, the part of the sentence in parenthesis ('the exhaustion...') may not be called a *statement* in the proper sense. Yet, if so, this only shows the irrelevance of the category 'statement' in my view: There exist apparently many propositions that cannot be called 'statements' but which are very important for our lives (as the example of the climate-changes is). Thus, whether they are called statements or not, we must find ways to deal with them in a rational fashion. If we cannot do so along bivalent lines, then we have to try a different, non-bivalent route.

I hope not to have misconstrued Brümmer's point. If not, I would like to challenge him by asking what is wrong with the above example. In my view, neither bivalence nor *tertium non datur* are in any way necessary requirements for the success of speech acts.

Regarding *van Woudenberg's* response, I am positive that he and I mean different things when discussing bivalence: He suggests that my view is that propositions A and B can both be true although A entails not B. He continues that in 'this way lies madness' and that 'that way we legitimize nonsensical talk'.

I agree with van Woudenberg about the madness charge. But this charge applies to (some) postmodernist views *but not to mine*. I do *not* hold that A and B can both be true although B entails not A. The reason is that 'truth is one' (see section 1).

Yet, I *do* hold that cases can exist in which deviant propositions can be held simultaneously in a legitimate fashion. Yet, the reason is not that both are true but that the speakers who make those propositions can both be justified to do so (given their different contexts; for a fuller treatment of the issue of justification, see section 9).

## 5. *Bivalence and exclusivist competitions*

The main reason why I discuss the notions of bivalence and *tertium non datur* that extensively here is that some of the respondents have hammered on them. Yet, in this particular context, *I* am not so much concerned with them, at least, not with them as *logical* notions. Rather, my prime concern is with a *consequence* they imply: Bivalent concepts of truth entail an 'either/or' in the strict, i.e. *exclusivist* sense of the word. Within a bivalent frame of reference, legitimacy ('truth') is *either* predicated of A *or* of B. That is, if A is legitimate then B *must* be illegitimate (provided it relates to A in the ways specified by van Woudenberg and Brümmer[30]). A bivalent logic thus implies that the *competition between A and B is an exclusivist* one. This exclusivist character of the competition[31] is my prime concern in this context, i.e. the context of discussing the issue of religious diversity.

I will first flesh out what I mean by 'exclusivist kinds of competitions' in three short points. Then, I will explain why I regard them to be counterproductive in the context of discussing religious diversity towards the end of this section.

First, exclusivist competitions rule out the possibility of grading legitimacy. They rule out, e.g. the possibility that both A and B are legitimate but that they are legitimate to different degrees. Construed within an exclusivist frame of reference, 'legitimacy' behaves like 'truth' does within a bivalent frame: In both cases, it does not make sense to suggest 'A is true/legitimate and B is true/legitimate to a lesser extent' (see also van Woudenberg on this point).

Second, illegitimacy ('falsity') is determined on a priori grounds under exclusivist parameters. By that I mean that B's illegitimacy ('falsity') is not determined after having carefully scrutinized it but simply by virtue of the fact that B relates to A in a certain fashion: If A is considered to be legitimate ('true') and B relates to A in a particular fashion, I do not need to know more about B. I can tell right away that it must be illegitimate ('false') under exclusivist parameters.

Third, B's illegitimacy ('falsity') is not only determined on a priori grounds but also by way of a strict *necessity*[32]: Holding A *obliges* me to consider B to be illegitimate ('false') by necessity, i.e. independently of contingent factors, such as psychological ones. No matter what my personality or my (religious) outlook is like, whether I happen to be a particularly stubborn or mild-mannered person, a (religious or anti-religious) fanatic or not, I *have to* consider B to be illegitimate ('false'). Even if it were my heart's desire not to do so, I would still be obliged to do so. This is simply a consequence of the logic implied in exclusivist competitions: Once I hold A, I *cannot* fail to consider B to be illegitimate ('false'). *Failing* to do so would reveal that I do not truly consider A to be legitimate ('true') or, else, have implicitly abrogated exclusivism or a bivalent frame of reference.

In sum, my concern with bivalence and *tertium non datur* is that they imply a particular consequence, viz. an exclusivist kind of competition. Different from other, more benign forms of competitions, *exclusivist competitions imply a necessary displacement relation on a priori grounds*: If A is considered to be legitimate or 'true', B must be displaced as a matter of necessity and on *a priori* grounds.

This displacement relation is obviously a *prima facie* one. By that I mean that it is not ruled out there may exist overriding reasons why we should not displace B under certain circumstances. For example, we can construe the notion of tolerance in such a strong fashion that it overrides the *prima facie* pull towards displacing B. I will discuss the nature of this pull and the problems implied in construing the notion of tolerance in a strong fashion below (see sections 7 and 8).

Yet, for now, I wish to emphasize a different point, viz. that such a displacement relation is fatal for a constructive discourse on religious diversity: Postulating necessary and a priori displacement relations between the deviant religious (sets of) beliefs A and B rules out a serious interreligious dialogue from the beginning on. If I consider your deviant religious beliefs B to be illegitimate ('false'), I have no reason to try to understand your religion in the 'deep' fashion which I fleshed out in my inaugural lecture. For example, I have no reason to 'mirror' my religious beliefs in light of yours. Nor do I have reason to consider your religious beliefs to be a serious challenge to my own which invites me to reflect more thoroughly on my own religious beliefs. After all, who would want to learn from falsity, who would consider alternative religious beliefs to be a serious challenge to his own if he knows that they are illegitimate or even false? As long as I assume that your religious beliefs are illegitimate or even false, I have no reason to engage in the activities which characterize a serious interreligious dialogue.

My point is thus that we have to provide a different frame of reference than an exclusivist competition if we wish to engage in an interreligious dialogue which is a true *dialogue*. In order to do so, we have to let go of the displacement relation between deviant (sets of) religious beliefs. At least, we have to let go of the a priori and necessary character of this displacement relation.

*This* is the background why I reject the notions of bivalence and *tertium non datur*. I see them giving rise to an exclusivist competition implying an a priori and necessary displacement relation between deviant beliefs. Since I reject this kind of competition, I reject those notions as well.

Yet, nothing hangs on the use of those notions as such. If my critics can demonstrate that bivalence and *tertium non datur* do *not* lead to an exclusivist competition, I will be happy to retreat from my criticism of those notions. The same is true if my critics could show that other notions than those two are primarily responsible for conceptualizing the competition between deviant religious beliefs in terms of an exclusivist competition. If so, I would leave those notions for what they are and target those other notions.

## 6. *Exclusivist competitions and a Dawkinian attitude: atheism, a license to kill?*

In this section, I will provide the reasons why I reject exclusivist competitions with their a priori and necessary displacement relation. Since I think that they can lead to morally and politically highly dangerous consequences, I will reject them in strong terms.

Yet, before I begin criticizing them, I would like to point out that I do not regard exclusivist competitions to be superfluous or dangerous in all realms of inquiry. In certain realms, the beliefs implied are of such a sort that they lend themselves to being treated within bivalent parameters, thus as exclusivist competitors. An example is the belief that the traffic light is red. In cases like this one, it is perfectly legitimate to construe the beliefs at stake in terms of a displacement relation: If I hold the belief that it is red and my discussion partner that it is not, I have the right to displace her false belief (given certain conditions[33]).

Yet, the question is whether *all* differences should be construed in terms of an exclusivist competition. Shall we construe, say, all cultural and religious differences along the lines of such a displacement relation? At this point, two fundamentally different attitudes, two different ways of being in the world, are possible. The first is the *anti-exclusivist* one. It can, e.g. be based upon the insights generated in the last century in philosophy (of science) and other meta-disciplines which foster (self-)critical reflection. They have made the historicity of our own standpoints abundantly clear. They have demonstrated that the meta-resources with the help of which we legitimize our standpoints are not time-lessly valid, not absolutely 'objective', but time-bound and contingent.

This does not mean that one meta-resource would be as good as the other. Thus, those insights do not necessarily imply a relativism. Yet, they imply that holding a worldview or defending particular meta-resources should be accompanied by a certain attitude. This attitude is one of *(self-)critique which acknowledges the historicity of one's own stand-points and the possibility that different standpoints may in principle be legitimate as well.*

The opposite position is an attitude which is characterized by a lack of (self-)critical thinking and the denial of any raison d'etre to diverging standpoints. *The* very current representatives of this kind of attitude are in my view people such as Richard *Dawkins*. They lack any consciousness of the historicity of their own positions and are thus incapable or unwilling to question them in a self-critical spirit. The consequence is that they consider all deviating positions to be 'false' or to be epistemically inferior to their own position. I call the attitude with the help of which Dawkins and Co. hold their positions a Dawkinian attitude or, in short, *Dawkinianism*.

More precisely, Dawkinianism is characterized by the following sets of beliefs:

- 'There is one truth and I or my group (say, crude naturalists[34]) possess it.'
- 'All deviating views are false/epistemically inferior and need, at least, in principle, to be displaced by my (our) true beliefs.'

Holding both of those beliefs goes often hand in hand with 'explanations' why other people hold inferior beliefs. Those 'explanations' are not strictly necessary for Dawkinianism but help to satisfy the human curiosity why other people hold false beliefs:

- 'They are not as bright[35] as I (Dawkins) am or we (say, crude naturalists) are since they do not base their beliefs upon evidence…'

Dawkinianism implies thus a strong form of exclusivism: It construes differences in terms of an exclusivist competition according to which all beliefs which differ from their own need to be displaced.

Holding beliefs in a Dawkinian attitude can entail morally highly questionable consequences: It can *license fanaticism*. If you really think that there is only one truth and you or your group are the only ones who possess it, there is a good chance that you will battle all different beliefs as fanatically as Dawkins does. This will particularly be the case if you combine the perception of difference with epistemic value judgments, as Dawkins and Co.

do: In their eyes, the reason that other people hold different beliefs is that those people are epistemically deficient. They do not use evidence, or do not use it in a 'scientific' fashion,[36] are not as bright as Dawkins and Co. themselves are, etc. If you truly think this way – i.e. if it is more than a clever marketing strategy – you will tend to think that you have the right to displace other people's beliefs. You will probably even think that you have a *duty* to preach them your naturalist, atheist, or whatever gospel you happen to hold.

Worse, Dawkinian fanatics often direct their aggression not only against what they consider to be false or inferior beliefs but also against the *people* who hold those beliefs. Dawkins' favorite doctrine, atheism, is probably the most pertinent recent example for that: The history of the twentieth century witnesses to atheism's readiness to eradicate not only (what it considers to be) false beliefs, religious ones being at the top of its list, but also the people who hold those beliefs. Stalin is only one example.[37] The first comprehensive large-scale experiments in the twentieth century have demonstrated that, under certain circumstances, *atheism is a license to kill.*

My point is *not* that all forms of atheism are as brutish as Stalin's was nor that all forms of exclusivist competitions are pursued as fanatically as Dawkins' exclusivism is. Yet, there is a slippery slope from exclusivist competitions to holding a Dawkinian attitude to fanaticism to becoming a license to kill. Under certain historical circumstances, one can lead to the other. In order to avoid getting us onto this slope in the first place, I suggest that we should proceed very cautiously when taking the first step, whereas this step consists in construing differences in terms of exclusivist competitions with their a priori and necessary displacement relations. In so far as the principles of bivalence and *tertium non datur* give rise to this sort of exclusivism, we should be cautious about their use as well.

## Tolerance

### 7. *Exclusivist competitions and tolerance*

I will now turn to the relationship between exclusivist kinds of competitions and an issue the respondents have emphasized, viz. tolerance. The above considerations on exclusivist kinds of competitions allow to take a fresh look on the issue of tolerance in my view.

Let me raise an admittedly very provocative question right at the beginning: *Is tolerance more than only some kind of repair kit for exclusivists?* Put more moderately: Does the notion of tolerance gain most of its importance from exclusivist presuppositions? Thus, if we let go of those presuppositions, as I suggest here, will this notion lose much of its importance? The answer provided at the end of this section will be a nuanced affirmation. But before I come to that I will explain what I mean by those questions.

As demonstrated above, exclusivist kinds of competitions imply a necessary displacement relation between (certain kinds of) deviant beliefs on a priori grounds. In the following, I will call this a *pull towards displacing deviant beliefs.*

The notion of tolerance gains much of its importance thanks to this pull. It is a countermeasure to neutralize it. Once this pull is in place but we do not wish to succumb to it – say, we have overriding political or cultural reasons for not displacing deviant beliefs – we have to introduce countermeasures, tolerance being one of them. Yet, if there were no such pull in the first place, there would be no necessity to introduce such countermeasures, there would be no need – or much less of a need (see below) – to introduce notions such as tolerance.

I will explain this point with the help of a comparison: Think of a car with an automatic transmission which is in gear. It has a tendency to pull forward. If we do not wish it to go forward – say, because we are at a stop light – we have to take counter-measures. For example, we have to engage the brake. Thus, the necessity to take counter-measures emerges only because the car has this tendency to move forward. If it had not, there would be no need to engage the brakes, thus, no need to take countermeasures.

The point of comparison is that tolerance is a countermeasure such as engaging the brakes is which is necessary only because we have created this pull in the first place. As it is necessary to engage the brakes only because the car has this tendency to move forward it is necessary to tolerate deviant beliefs only because of the tendency to displace them.

However, if we view things this way, the following questions suggest themselves: 'Why leave the car in gear at all if we do not wish it to move forward (say, while waiting at a traffic light)? Why not put it in neutral instead so that it does not pull forward anymore?' Does it not suggest itself to avoid this pull in the first place rather than, first, creating it only to, second, neutralize it? *No pull forward, no necessity to take countermeasures.*

Can this motto be transferred to the issue at stake here? If so it would go as follows: *No pull towards displacing deviant beliefs, no necessity to be tolerant.* If we would avoid the pull towards displacing false beliefs in the first place, we would be relieved from the necessity to introduce countermeasures. We would not have to spend energy on construing strenuous notions of tolerance (see section 8). Rather than solving a self-created problem by strenuous means, why not avoid the problem in the first place?

Let me alert you to the fact that, once the pull towards displacing deviant beliefs is created, we are not only under *any* kind of obligation to introduce countermeasures but under an obligation to introduce measures which are strong enough to neutralize this pull. Thus, this pull and the countermeasures must be *balanced* against each other. The stronger the pull, the stronger the countermeasure must be.

I will explain this point by taking up the example of the car which is in gear again: If this car has a strong engine, its brakes must be strong enough to be capable of countering the strong pull it exerts. If they are not strong enough, the car will move forward in spite of our efforts to break its forward-pull. Thus, the strength of the brakes must be adjusted to the strength of the engine. There must thus be a balance.

Such a balance is necessary as well when construing countermeasures for the purposes of neutralizing the pull towards displacing false beliefs: If there is a strong pull, the countermeasures taken must be strong as well. For example, if we introduce a notion of tolerance as such a countermeasure, it must be construed strong enough to do the job. If it is not, it cannot break the pull towards displacing deviant beliefs.

I will illustrate this point with the help of an argument Dawkins provides. Let me say for the sake of clarity that, as much as I disagree with him on other occasions, he has a point on this particular issue.

When discussing why the Amish are allowed to prevent their children from going to school, Dawkins suggests that the reason for this is that we (respectively the U.S. culture) wish to enrich 'human diversity'.[38] Following a like-minded spirit, N. Humphrey, he points out that it is *third parties*, in this case the children of the Amish, who pay the price for our ideal to enrich cultural diversity: The children of the Amish are deprived of a decent education.[39] Not surprisingly, Dawkins and Humphrey reject this Amish practice.

My point is neither to support Dawkins's reconstruction of the issue nor to take a stance on the Amish practice of preventing their children from going to school. Dawkins misconstrues the issue at stake[40] and fails to appreciate the historical background upon which the Amish practice rests.[41] Yet, what he succeeds in (inadvertently) is to point to the necessity of balancing whatever countermeasure is taken against the pull to displace false beliefs. If it were truly nothing else but our desire to enrich cultural diversity, this countermeasure would not neutralize the pull towards displacing the Amish beliefs (respectively the practice based upon those beliefs). The countermeasure 'desire to enrich cultural diversity' cannot outweigh the harm the Amish practice causes. This harm consists of depriving the Amish children of a decent education. In order to outweigh it, more is needed than high-flying ideals such as 'enriching cultural diversity'. This is particularly so since the harm affects others, not the people who hold those ideals: It is the *children of the Amish*, not the people who hold those high-flying ideals who pay the price for those ideals.

In sum, once we create a pull towards displacing deviant beliefs, we are under an obligation to construe countermeasures which are strong enough to neutralize this pull, if we do not wish to succumb to it. There must be a balance between the strength of the pull and the strength of the countermeasures suggested. Yet, construing strong countermeasures is a very strenuous affair and, as will become clear below (see section 8), construing the notion of tolerance in a strong fashion harbors serious moral and political risks.

The main purpose of this section is to point to the conceptual link between exclusivist competitions and the notion of tolerance. This is in so far part of the overall argument as it was demonstrated above that exclusivism is related to bivalence/*tertium non datur*. Thus, this section shows that the concept of tolerance is based upon very particular presuppositions, viz. an exclusivism and a bivalent frame of reference. I take this insight to be interesting, possibly novel, and it may help to re-conceptualize the notion of tolerance and the appreciation it commonly receives. This will be particularly the case if you are as skeptical about exclusivism (and bivalence/*tertium non datur*) as I am. If so, you will relativize the importance of the notion of tolerance.

Yet, my point is only to *relativize* the importance of this notion, *not* to abrogate it. I wish to provoke the widespread acceptance and sometimes uncritical appreciation of tolerance. Yet, once this is achieved, I am ready to admit that we cannot do without tolerance. Even if we would abandon exclusivist kinds of competitions with their necessary and a priori displacement relations, *some* notion of tolerance will still be necessary. After all, even if exclusivism is abandoned, there is *some* kind of competition left between deviant beliefs. Even if I have skipped the idea that my (religious) beliefs displace yours by necessity and on a priori grounds, our (religious) beliefs still compete with each other to some extent. I *still disagree* with your (religious) beliefs (and if I would not, I should consider converting to your religion).

Yet, this disagreement will be of a different kind than a disagreement on exclusivist grounds (I will flesh this difference out in section 11). If I do not consider a deviant (religious) belief to be illegitimate or false, my reasons for disagreeing with it will be less strong than under exclusivist or bivalent parameters. Thus, the pull to displace those deviant beliefs will be not as strong as under those parameters. Consequently, the countermeasures which are required for neutralizing it do not have to be construed as strongly as under those parameters. We thus do not need as strenuous a notion of tolerance as we would need under exclusivist parameters. I consider that to be an advantage in the face of the problems strong notions of tolerance harbor, as I will show in the following section.

## 8. *Tolerance and unjustified religious belief (Peter Jonkers)*

In this section, I will take up Jonkers' approach towards tolerance. The reason that I delve that deeply into it is that it is (in my view) representative of a certain kind of Continental thinking with which I have an ambiguous relation: On the one hand, I appreciate it for its acknowledgment of the possibility of deep-going and probably irreconcilable difference. This is the very point of the justified difference approach I favor, viz. to provide a theoretical conceptualization of this possibility. Also, Continental thinkers often take more strongly into account comprehensive themes, such as questions of the *conditio humana*, than Anglo-American thinkers with their emphasis upon 'dry' (epistemo)logical issues.

On the other hand, however, I think that Continental thinkers are not always entirely clear on what they mean precisely. In my view, this is not because they would be incapable of writing more clearly but because they value other things, such as style and the effect, more highly than argumentative precision. As long as they restrict themselves to contributing to literary genres or something of that sort, this may be legitimate. Yet, if they intend to contribute to moral or political issues, this lack of clarity is disturbing since it can give rise to misunderstandings.

In Jonkers' case, I wonder whether he intends his strong emphasis upon tolerance to function as a moral guideline for political action. If so, what would this imply in political terms? For example, what would it imply for policy-making in Europe, Europe being currently challenged by large numbers of refugees most of whom have very different religious, cultural, intellectual, and political values than most Europeans have? What political consequences would follow if we would use Jonkers' far-going emphasis upon tolerance as a basis for political decision-making?

Or are Jonkers' suggestions not to be understood as politically relevant contentions? If not, what else is their purpose? Does he wish to point to larger philosophical or religious issues, such as to the *conditio humana*, rather than to provide reasons for political action?

Although the notion of tolerance does not play as important a role in my account as it does in Jonkers' account, I still wish to press him on this point. The reason is that the issue of tolerance is a morally and politically highly relevant one and we should be utterly clear what we mean when we use it. This is why I will consider in the following two possible ways to understand Jonkers' contribution and will invite him at the end to clarify his position.

*Jonkers* criticizes my contentions because they avoid what he considers to be the very issue that matters in the discussion on religious differences. This is the question how to deal with *un*justified differences. Following Ricoeur, Jonkers relates this question to the notion of tolerance: The kind of tolerance Jonkers (and Ricoeur) favor 'entitles individuals and collectivities to hold on to (the truth of) their religious values and practices, whether or not these are justified in the eyes of others…'

On pain of appearing to be simple-minded, burgeois, or whatever in some Continental eyes, I have a very simple response to positions like this: *We should not tolerate that which is unjustified*.

Obviously, this response needs to be qualified in order to be brought into a fruitful dialogue with Jonkers' position. It depends on what we mean by 'tolerance' as well as by 'unjustified'. I will begin by discussing the latter notion.

I understand Jonkers to mean by 'unjustified' (sets of) beliefs which are false. An example is the above-mentioned belief that the traffic light is green whereas it is red.[42] If somebody holds the view that it is green whereas it is red, I will not tolerate her unjustified belief. And, frankly, I see no reason why I should try to bring myself to tolerate it. If Jonkers suggests that I should, I strongly disagree with him.

The same goes for the example provided in my inaugural lecture, viz. that of the racist. Say, he holds the belief that the Aryan race is genetically superior to other races. For all we can tell, this belief is unjustified since it is false. This is an example of a belief which is in Jonkers' terminology 'objectionable or…repulsive'. But different from Jonkers, I see no reason why I should try to bring myself to tolerate beliefs of this sort.

Obviously, the plausibility of this response depends upon what we mean by 'tolerance'. More precisely speaking, it depends upon the context in which we exercise tolerance. I think that a basic distinction regarding the contexts in which we exercise tolerance is that between contexts which are highly action-relevant and those which are not. I will begin by discussing the latter.

An example of a relatively action-*ir*relevant context is the arts. Say, I visit a museum of arts with a friend and she holds that the color of a painting is red whereas it is green. I may 'tolerate' her deviating beliefs because nothing much hangs on them. And I grant that even racist beliefs or expressions may be tolerable in artistic and related contexts (think, e.g. of Anselm Kiefer's use of Nazi-symbolism in some of his artistic works).

Yet, things are different when we have it over action-relevant contexts. For example, I will not be prepared to tolerate my friend's deviating views on red and green when she drives a car. Too much is at stake in this context. Put more generally: In highly action-relevant contexts, we should be much more cautious with exercising tolerance.

How do Jonkers's suggestions that we should 'start from the experience of the intolerable' and that 'paradoxically, the notion of the intolerable is essential for tolerance' fit into this distinction? If I understand him correctly, Jonkers means those remarks to be some kind of general characterization of tolerance, a sort of litmus test for it. Yet, I wonder whether Jonkers would be prepared to hold that those characterizations hold in *all* contexts, including action-relevant ones. Does he, e.g. seriously wish to suggest that we should tolerate the actions of the (young) male immigrants who assaulted women in Cologne and elsewhere on New Year's Eve 2015?

My question to Jonkers is thus what kind of issues he wishes to target, into what kind of genre his suggestions belong. In the first couple of pages, he hammers on issues such as 'the burning questions that contemporary society asks about the role of religion in the public space', 'the reality of concrete (conflicting) practices', etc. Here, it seems that he wishes to contribute to action-relevant fields, such as political theory or morality or the (philosophical and religious) reflections on them. If taken to contribute to strongly action-relevant fields of this sort, I flatly reject Jonkers' advocacy of such a strong notion of tolerance.

Yet, towards the end of his paper, Jonkers has it over 'heuristic function(s)', 'the sting' of 'the vexing question of tolerance', a 'point of resistance against the erosion of tolerance', and 'our moral responsibility regarding our vulnerability to all kinds of harms'. I take those remarks to point in the direction of less action-relevant fields, to, say reflections on the *conditio humana*. If *this* is what he truly means, my disagreement with his approach to tolerance is *not* as great as I have suggested above.

In sum, I invite Jonkers to specify further towards which sorts of contexts his advocacy of such a strong notion of tolerance is geared. Does he have action-relevant contexts in mind nor not?

**Justification and 'justified difference'**

*9. A discussion on justification and 'justified difference'*

My primary goal in the inaugural lecture is to develop an intellectually and philosophically respectable foundation upon which a constructive theory of religious diversity can be built (what I call the paradigm of 'justified religious difference'). This foundation is the theory of alterity I suggest, viz. 'justified difference'. The notion of justification is obviously part and parcel of it. Yet, it is only a *means* to achieve another end, viz. that of providing this foundation. If it should turn out that this end is better served by other means, I will be happy to use *them* rather than the notion of justification.

In principle, a number of different routes could be pursued after the acknowledgment that the principle of bivalence and exclusivism lead into a dead end for the purposes of dealing constructively with the issue of religious diversity. One such route is to substitute a bivalent logic by a many-valued logic, as Margolis suggests. The reason why I have not pursued this route here[43] is that relying on a many-valued logic implies remaining on the syntactic level, i.e. on the level of beliefs only (since logical relations hold only between beliefs). Reliance on the concept of justification, however, allows us to get further than that by getting *agents holding beliefs* into picture as well.[44] Getting agents holding beliefs into picture, thus the 'pragmatic dimension', is in line with promising current developments in epistemology along pragmatic lines, such as attempts to establish a 'virtue epistemology'.

Wolterstorff's concept of 'entitlement'[45] would be another alternative: It would allow to get the pragmatic dimension into picture. Yet, the reason why I have finally decided to favor 'justification' over 'entitlement' is that the former has been connected in explicit ways to the issues which are of utmost relevance to my further argument, viz. that of context-dependency and (epistemic) perspectivalism. I will turn to both issues now.

Regarding the issue of context-dependency, I think of the discussion on the differences between the notions of justification and that of truth as pursued in the 'neo-pragmatist' tradition. For example, Rorty insists that justification is context-dependent in a way in which truth is not.[46] As much as I disagree with Rorty on other occasions, I think that this distinction makes good sense. And the same goes for Jeffrey Stout's suggestion that 'being justified in believing something – being entitled to believe it – is a status that can vary from context to context'.[47] Whether an agent is justified to believe something thus depends on her (epistemic) circumstances.

Regarding the issue of *perspectivalism*, I think of the recent discussion in epistemology on the question under what circumstances an agent is justified to hold the beliefs she holds. In particular, I think of the discussion to what extent agents and the circumstances under which they believe should be idealized. For example, Jonathan Kvanvig criticizes accounts which idealize those circumstances and suggests that we should rely on the de facto circumstances under which agents come to hold their beliefs. Yet, if we do, 'justification is perspectival'.[48] That is, whether epistemic justification obtains depends on 'the facts about a believer's cognitive situation....'[49] Kvanvig suggests thus that 'what a person is justified in believing right now depends crucially on that person's *perspective*...[it] depends on the information that person has...[and] not the information a virtuous person in those circumstances would possess exercising their exalted epistemic talents in those circumstances'.[50]

For our purposes, the most important upshot of both rounds of discussion is that justification is plural: Relying on de facto agents rather than idealized ones implies the existence of a plurality of legitimate perspectives. Those perspectives can be as legitimately different as the agents can be legitimately different. And acknowledging that justification is context-dependent has the same result: Justification can be as legitimately different as the (cognitive and related) contexts within which it is pursued can be legitimately different. In sum, *justification being context-dependent and perspectival can be legitimately different, thus can be plural.*

This *pluralism of justification is the key to the 'justified difference'-approach* I suggest: A justification of a belief, A, within a particular context and/or perspective may, at least, in principle be as legitimate as a justification of a deviant belief, B, is within a different context and/or perspective. More precisely speaking, that A is legitimate does not rule out the possibility that B is legitimate as well. It certainly does not rule out this possibility on a priori or necessary grounds, as exclusivist kinds of competitions do.

In sum, *justification pluralized, thus* the concept of *justified difference, is the theoretical counterpart to exclusivist kinds of competitions with their necessary and* a priori *displacement relation between A and B*. It allows for the possibility that *both* A and B can be justified.

Please note that I mean the term 'possibility' in a strict sense: All I have argued for thus far is that it is *not necessarily and on* a priori *grounds impossible* that B can be legitimate although A has been recognized as being legitimate. I emphasize this possibility because exclusivist kinds of competitions and bivalence/*tertium non datur*, in so far as they give rise to exclusivism, rule it out.

Yet, nothing has been said about the conditions under which A and B can both be legitimate, e.g. whether it is possible that both are legitimate, but to different degrees. My point here is not to provide a scheme for distinguishing between degrees of legitimacy[51] but to provide a theoretical framework *within which difference can be conceptualized* at all. Thus, I wish to provide a framework which allows for the *possibility to think difference*, possibly of an irreducible sort, in a coherent fashion.

But although primarily of a theoretical nature, this framework has action-relevant consequences: As I will demonstrate below, the interaction with a disagreeable belief which is legitimate is different than the interaction with a disagreeable belief which is *il*legitimate or false. Most importantly, the interaction with a *person* holding disagreeable beliefs which are legitimate is different than the interaction with a person holding disagreeable beliefs which are illegitimate (see section 11).

### 10. *Pihlström's, van den Brom's, and van Woudenberg's challenges of my use of the notion of justification*

Pihlström, van den Brom, and van Woudenberg have raised important questions and challenges concerning my use of the notion of justification. I cannot answer all of them in the remaining space but will take up some of the most urgent ones in the following.

*Pihlström* asks whether I propose that deviant religious beliefs *are* justified or *can be* justified. After what I mentioned in the previous section, it is obvious that I only argue that they *can* be justified, not that they are. As indicated, I just wish to secure the *basic possibility* that there can be such a thing as legitimate differences between religious beliefs.

Securing this possibility is a necessary requirement for a theory of alterity worth its name. Frankly, I see no other responsible[52] way to do so. Certainly, the notion of (non-pluralizable) truth will not do. If you take truth of a bivalent sort as a basis and proceed along exclusivist lines, you will end up with a different thing than the theory of alterity I have in mind. Inevitably, you will end up with the pattern identified above (see section 7), viz. a pull towards displacing deviant beliefs which then, in a second step, needs to be neutralized, say, by introducing a notion of tolerance.

But this pattern is not only very strenuous but also insufficient for the purposes of developing the paradigm of 'justified religious difference'. For example, it would fail to account for a concept of the interreligious dialogue worth its name. It fails to account for activities such as re-considering my religious beliefs in light of your deviant religious beliefs, 'mirroring' my beliefs in light of yours, etc. If I consider your deviant religious beliefs to be illegitimate or false, they do not provide a serious challenge to mine nor would I want to 'mirror' my religious beliefs in light of yours. The notion of tolerance does not provide any solace at this point: No matter how much I tolerate your deviant religious beliefs and what consequences this may have in the political realm, as long as I consider them to be false, I have no reason to learn from them.

In sum, a foundation built upon a *non-pluralizable notion of truth or some other kind of exclusivist competition seriously underdetermines a robust theory of alterity as well as the paradigm of justified religious difference.* In order to get both of them off the ground, a foundation is necessary which *is* pluralizable. This is my principal point. If we agree on it, the rest is negotiable: Whether we think that a pluralizable basis can best be fleshed-out by means of a many-valued logics, the notion of entitlement, or justification, or whatever else may come to mind is just a matter of strategical considerations.

This point is related to my answer to *van den Brom's* criticism: He regards my account of justification to be too abstract. He proposes that …'the justification of a deviant epistemological perspective would only make sense in the case of a concrete particular perspective, i.e.… [a] perspective from *within* a particular faith' (my italics).

I agree with van den Brom's point that delving into the inside-perspective of a religion is crucial when determining concrete criteria for the purposes of distinguishing between religious differences that are justified and those that are not. Speaking for my own religion, I think, e.g. of the complex dialectics that characterizes Christian eschatology: On the one hand, Jesus the Christ is the *arrabon*, the down-payment for the eschaton. Yet, on the other hand, the eschaton is not yet realized and the knowledge about it is imperfect (see 1. Corinthians 13:12). This dialectics turned cognitively – we are not completely ignorant about the ultimate Truth but would be utterly presumptuous to assume that we have it at our disposal *hic et nunc* – seems to me to be a promising point of departure for dealing constructively with religious diversity.

Yet, before (*logically* 'before') we can delve into our respective religious inside-perspectives, we first need to secure the theoretical *possibility* that there can be such a phenomenon as 'justified religious difference' (or whatever you want to call it). We thus need some kind of viable meta-perspective which helps to create the proper conceptual space within which difference can be 'negotiated' (to say things in current parlance). *This is what the account of 'justified difference' I suggest is supposed to achieve.* Since this account has a different function from the move of delving into the religious inside-perspectives, I see no need to play off one against the other.[53]

*Van Woudenberg* raises a number of issues concerning my use of the notion of justification. One concern which I take to be crucial for him is the question whether my reference to justification is pursued in a spirit critical of religion.

It is *absolutely not.* Obviously, working in an environment which is as aggressively secularized as the Dutch one, one must be careful with religious 'coming outs'. Yet, it is quite obvious for anybody who has followed my writings on justification that their driving intention is an apologetic one. My reconstructions of William James's 'Will to Believe' as a (successful!) apologetic argument for being justified to hold one's religious beliefs witness to that.[54]

On the more technical side, *van Woudenberg* raises the issue of internal versus external justification. At least, that is how I interpret his remarks on the de facto reliable belief-forming mechanisms (see above). Yet, if (epistemological) *internalism* is characterized as agents being justified when they have fulfilled their epistemic obligations, I reject internalism. Even if the perpetrators were subjectively justified to publicly assault women in Cologne and elsewhere on New Year 's Eve 2015 – maybe they did not know any better, given the concept of womanhood they were raised with – I still think that they were not justified to do what they have done.

Yet, if (epistemological) *externalism* is characterized as the view that a belief is justified when based upon reliable belief-forming mechanisms, I am skeptical about it as well. First of all, the discussion on what mechanisms are reliable has turned in our age and (Western) culture into some kind of power game: It is dominated by empiricists laying down their laws on all other domains of inquiry. Second, even if some unbiased criteria for determining the reliability of belief-generating mechanisms could be developed, it would still not necessarily be the case that only beliefs formed by them are justified all things considered. As James's arguments have made abundantly clear, we can be perfectly justified to hold beliefs which are generated by relatively unreliable mechanisms, if there are overriding reasons to do so.[55]

Thus, if specified as above, I subscribe neither to externalism nor to internalism.[56] In my view, the distinction between them is one of those classical epistemological classifications which have only limited value. At least, for the issue under consideration, this distinction is not very helpful.

## 11. *'Justified difference': towards a robust theory of alterity*

Although the respondents have not raised many questions about the specifics of the account of 'justified difference' I suggest, I would nevertheless like to take this opportunity to spell it out more extensively than I could do in my inaugural lecture.

My main issue is to distinguish between different kinds of disagreements. I think that it makes a significant difference whether I disagree with a (set of) belief(s) on the grounds that it is *il*legitimate or false and on the grounds that it is *not* illegitimate or false. Thus, I think it makes a difference whether I disagree with your belief, x, on the ground

(A) that x is false

or

(B) On the ground that I do *not* consider x to be false (say, because the evidence is not sufficient to consider x to be false) but have other reasons to do so.

I will explain this difference with the help of an example chosen from the field of environmental ethics. The following background information is crucial for understanding the point I wish to make with the help of this example: To my knowledge, there is good evidence to suggest that the exhaustion of carbon dioxides is responsible for the current changes of the climate. Yet, *the extent* to which it is responsible for this change is contested: There is some evidence suggesting that it is responsible for it to a *significant* extent but this evidence is not (yet) conclusive.[57]

Now, say, somebody holds the belief

(C) 'The exhaustion of carbon dioxides is not responsible for the current climate-change'

whereas another person holds the belief

(D) 'The exhaustion of carbon dioxides is not *to a significant extent* responsible for the current climate-change'.

I disagree with both C and D. Yet, the reasons why I disagree with them are different: Regarding proposition C, I would be prepared to hold that it is (or comes close to being) plainly false. Yet, I do not consider D to be false in the same sense and my reasons for rejecting it are more complex. Let me unpack some of this complexity.

As indicated, there is *some* evidence that D is false but it is not conclusive. Yet, given how the discussion on this (and related) issues has been conducted, I expect more evidence for D's falsity to surface when more research on the issue is done. Another important reason for rejecting D is that, given what is at stake, we can better err on being overly cautious than on being negligent. More precisely speaking, given that

- We have to decide on D under a significant amount of uncertainty because we do not have the time to wait until all the relevant evidence concerning D is in (it may be too late by then)
- We are better off erring by sacrificing some of our economic growth for the reduction of carbon dioxides than erring by continuing with the *status quo* (which is to exhaust massive amounts of carbon dioxides in order to secure economic growth).

More reasons for rejecting D could be provided. Yet, my point is hopefully clear by now: It is that the reasons for rejecting D are much more complex than the straightforward rejection of C on the grounds that it is false.

Most importantly, my *attitude towards D and the person holding it* differs greatly from my attitude towards C and the person holding it: I reject C straightforwardly and will be, at least, on *prima facie* grounds be prepared to be critical about the mindset of the person holding it. I may, e.g. assume that he is ill-informed, is some kind of methodological purist, may even be suspicious that he is biased towards the exhaustion-intensive industry, and other such things. Consequently, I will not regard C to be a potential challenge to my own position nor as providing reasons to re-consider it. Rather, I will disregard it (at least, I have *prima facie* reasons to do so).

But my attitude towards D and the person holding it will be different. Although I disagree with D, I do not reject it as straightforwardly as I reject C. And I will not assume that the person holding it is ill-informed, a methodological purist, biased towards the exhaustion-intensive industry, etc.[58] Consequently, I will not disregard D as easily as I disregard C. Rather, I will regard it to be a *potential challenge to my own position*. For example, I may decide to read more on the issue, to read different kinds of literature than I have read thus far, listen and speak to different people than I have listened and spoken to thus far, etc.

That a deviant view provides a potential challenge to my own position does not necessarily mean that I will give up my own position in favor of it. Yet, it means that

I will reflect more (and, hopefully, more thoroughly[59]) on my own position. For example, I may reflect on the presuppositions of my own position and contrast them with the presuppositions upon which the deviant position rests. In this particular case, I may, e.g. assume that I have a different attitude towards the question how to act properly under uncertainty than the person holding D has. I may, e.g. assume that the person holding D is more of a risk-taker whereas I tend to act with greater caution under conditions of uncertainty. And/or I may assume that we have different value preferences: The person holding D values economic growth probably very highly whereas I prefer sacrificing some of our economic growth for the hope that this will benefit the world's climate.

There is much more to be said on this difference in attitude than I have said thus far. Yet, I would like to terminate the discussion here and summarize the point I wish to make: It is that disagreeing with D *entails a different attitude towards D and the person holding it* than disagreeing with C and the person holding it.

This difference is what I am after: I regard it to be a *promising basis upon which a (new) approach of alterity can be co*nstrued, viz. the 'justified difference' approach I favor. This approach should then serve as a foundation for the paradigm of 'justified religious difference' which allows for a constructive treatment of the issue of religious diversity.

The guiding idea is that (many of) our religious differences should be construed along the lines of my difference with D rather than along the lines of my difference with C: Although I disagree with a (set of) alternative religious belief(s), E, the mechanisms mentioned under D rather than those mentioned under C kick in: I will re-consider and 'mirror' my own religious beliefs in light of E. This does not mean that I will give up my own religious beliefs when exposed to E – at least, in most cases it does not. Yet, I will consider E to be a potential challenge to my own religious beliefs which makes me re-think them. Having exposed myself to the challenges E provides, I will return to my religious beliefs with a different, hopefully more reflected, consciousness.

I take it that this is the *proper foundation upon which an interreligious dialogue* worth its name *can flourish*. It cannot flourish if I consider your deviant religious beliefs to be false for the reasons mentioned above: No matter how much I tolerate your deviant religious beliefs – as long as I assume that they are illegitimate or false, I will not consider them to be a serious challenge to my own. Another way of putting the matter is to say that the notion of *tolerance is relatively irrelevant* for the purposes of providing proper conceptual space within which an interreligious dialogue can flourish.

Yet, what the notion of tolerance cannot achieve, the paradigm of 'justified religious difference' can: It allows to maintain (probably irreconcilable) difference between deviant religious beliefs but considers this *difference to be a discussion-starter rather than a discussion-stopper*. It is precisely this difference which provides the *raison d'etre* for entering into the interreligious dialogue.

Obviously, much more needs to be said on the difference and the communication between different religious points of view (and possible misunderstandings between them). I hope to be able to say more on it on another occasion. Yet, my point with this contribution is to lay the foundations – or providing help in doing so – upon which a concept of 'justified difference' can be built upon which, in turn, the paradigm of 'justified religious difference' can be erected. And I hope that my theses, sketchy as they are at this point, will provoke further (constructive) thoughts on the issue and will be happy to incorporate those thoughts into my own theses – in a critical spirit, if necessary.

## Acknowledgments

I would like to thank the five respondents for their thorough critique and am grateful for the opportunity to learn from the suggestions they made. Their critique provides an excellent opportunity for me to elaborate further on the paradigm of 'justified religious difference'. I feel particularly honored that people whom I consider to belong to the generation of my teachers are among the group of respondents.

## Disclosure statement

No potential conflict of interest was reported by the author.

## Notes

1. Van den Brom is conspicuously silent on my criticism of classical forms of religious pluralism. Yet, given his emphasis upon the necessity to delve into the particularities of particular traditions, I assume that he implicitly shares my criticism of Hick and others.
2. See above, *Pihlström*'s distinction between different sorts of positive attitudes towards other religions.
3. I mean 'Intentional' (with a capital 'I') as well as 'lingual' in Margolis' sense: Drawing on philosophical anthropology, e.g. Helmuth Plessner and Adolf Portmann, Margolis argue that intentionality and linguistic capabilities (including consciousness) *emerge* in the natural world but cannot be reduced to it in a materialist sense (see my Introduction in Pragmatism, xi–xiii).
4. See Rorty, *Philosophy*, 357–372 and my criticism in Empirisme, 331–332.
5. Frankly, I consider this assumption to be so natural that I would not even know what it would mean to seriously deny it. Thus, I understand attempts to think of a simultaneous existence of several worlds to be pure thought experiments or something of that sort (see, e.g. Goodman's *Ways of Worldmaking*).
6. The reason that somebody is justified to hold the belief x is because x is a good candidate for being true – rather than, say, that x is considered to be legitimate by the (Communist or whatever) party-doctrine (I will specify the notion of justification further below, see sections 9 and 10).
7. The issue that matters for people who are interested in developing a philosophy of religion which is hospitable to the pursuit of religion (as I am) is not *whether* 'ordinary' religious beliefs are reconstructed but in *what kind of sprit* they are reconstructed. For people like myself, the issue is whether or not they are reconstructed in a spirit which is sensitive to the 'logic' prevailing in religion.
8. Most recently, Trigg has defended a similar position in *Religious Diversity*.
9. A sub-variant of this rationalist line of argument are attempts to demonstrate that transcendent postulates have *transcendental* functions in the strict sense of the word, i.e. that they are a necessary presupposition for some other (crucial) activity. This sub-variant was (and is) widespread in the German-speaking context. For example, Paul Tillich suggests that '*God* is the presupposition of the question of God' ("Two Types," 290; italics mine). Yet, frankly, I doubt that van Woudenberg would feel comfortable in the neighborhood of approaches of this sort.
10. That no serious arguments speak against holding religious beliefs I take to be an adequate summary of the different arguments Plantinga provides in the different phases of his career. Even in his last phase, i.e. in *Warranted Christian Belief*, he does *not* attempt to demonstrate the truth of religious beliefs (I have pointed that out against common misunderstandings in "Plantingas Apologie", 974–975).
11. By 'the principle underlying it', I mean the suggestion that we should focus on the issue whether believers are justified to hold their beliefs rather than on the issue whether their beliefs are true. Yet, this does not mean that I subscribe to the way Plantinga works this suggestion out: In his earlier, second, phase, he endorses inadvertently a relativistic stance and the apologetic results of his last, third, phase are rather meager (see my "Plantingas Apologie", 979–980).
12. Although I do not have the space here to argue for it more extensively, I would at least like to mention in passing that 'truth' is used in the New Testament also in a different sense than what the philosophical notion of bivalence implies (see, e.g. John 16: 6).

13. I think, e.g. of Anthony Flew's "Presumption of Atheism" (in his earlier, atheist phase) which considers atheism to be the 'natural' position so that the onus of proof comes down on the shoulders of the theist (see his *God, Freedom, and Immortality*). Different from other atheists, Flew has to be credited with *explicitly reflecting* on the privileges he claims for atheism.

14. I think of the well-known atheist strategy to construe theism and atheism as being exclusive opposites, *tertium non datur*, and then to argue that theism fails (for this or that reason) so that atheism wins by default. The success of this strategy depends obviously on construing theism and atheism as exclusive opposites. The antidote to it is obvious: Introduce a third into the *tertium non datur* and atheism loses its default status. An obvious candidate four such a third is agnosticism which, if anything, can claim to possess default status.

   A particular mischievous sub-variant of this strategy is to smuggle atheism's default status into its definition: 'Atheism is the denial of theism'. Well, if it were that easy and substantial problems as that of (a)theism could be solved by definition, why not turn tables? Why not define theism as 'the denial of atheism' so that everything that is not arguably atheist is theist by default?

15. Feuerbach, Freud, and others draw unwarrantedly atheist conclusions from the argument that the religious belief-generating mechanisms are unreliable (the fact that a belief is based upon unreliable belief-generating mechanisms does not prove its falsity). Yet, I acknowledge that the charges that religion is based upon 'wishful thinking' or a 'projection' provide serious challenges for religious believers, once they are stripped from the peculiarities of Freud's and Feuerbach's accounts.

16. I think of criticisms such as that the judgments that God is (all)powerful and (all)loving are incompatible with the observation that there exists evil in this world. This criticism affects only *certain* religions and not religion per se. For example, religions which do not attribute powerfulness or lovingness to God are not affected by this criticism. Yet, those which are, such as certain sub-species of Christianity, have admittedly reasons to take this criticism seriously.

17. I think of classical Marxist and related criticisms of religions. Into this category fall also more recent accounts such as that of Nicholas Everitt ("The Non-Existence of God", 127) which speculate that 'if the world had been created by God, then we would have reasons to expect it to be x-like. Since it is not x-like, it is probably not created by God'. Obviously, this is highly speculative since many reasons can be conceived of why the world is not x-like. Everitt is honest enough to acknowledge this.

18. Another one is that agnosticism is in my view not a standpoint which suffices to guide one's life in an adequate manner. Yet, here, I will not elaborate on this issue further.

19. Different from above, 'semantics' is now used as a term of art within the discourse in formal logic.

20. Dummett, *Truth*, xxx.

21. See Margolis, *Pragmatism*, 118–123.

22. Margolis, *Historied Thought*, 65.

23. Although this is not my main concern here, I would like to mention in passing that the suggestion that reflections on truth are dependent upon the domain of inquiry at stake and how we think to be able to access it opens up new vistas for theology. Margolis demonstrates – convincingly, in my view – that the question what truth values are appropriate cannot be fixed in abstraction but depends upon the ontology and epistemology at stake (see Grube, "Margolis' Critique of Bivalence," 240–243). Insights of this sort can liberate theology and many human sciences from the methodological imperialism which has dominated them for decades (at least, in the Anglo-American world).

24. Please note that 'deviating' is logically weaker than Margolis' 'contradictory'. I do not wish to commit myself here wholeheartedly to Margolis' view that we should tolerate contradictory interpretations. Rather, I think that to what extent we can tolerate genuine contradictions depends on the domain of inquiry at stake, in particular, on its action-relevance: In relatively action-*ir*relevant domains, such as the arts, we may be able to tolerate contradictory interpretations more easily than in highly action-relevant ones, such as in religion.

25. See the criticism of this principle in Albert, *Traktat*, 12f et al.

26. See Russell, "On Denoting," 485–493.

27. See Rorty's criticism in "Fictional Discourse," 113.

28. From what I understand from van Woudenberg's discussion of it (see above), even the issue of justification has been abused to smuggle in an empiricist ideology.

29. For the complex relationship between insistence on bivalence and ontological and epistemo- logical questions, see Margolis, *The Truth*, 42–43, where he criticizes Wolterstorff).

30. Both A and B must be statements which genuinely contradict each other, etc. (see section 3).

31. I use 'exclusivism' here as a description for a particular kind of competition between deviant beliefs. Such a use is to be distinguished from the use of 'exclusivism' as one of three different ways to describe the relationships between the different religions ('exclusivism/inclusivism/ pluralism'). Here, I do not discuss the relation between the use of my term to the use of 'exclusivism' within the tripartite scheme. The reason is not only that this scheme is highly contested and more and more abandoned but, also, that it is rather complex: It implies, at least, a distinction between an exclusivism regarding claims to truth and an exclusivism regarding claims to salvation (see e.g. Robert McKim, *Religious Diversity*, 14–34 (regarding exclusivist claims to truth) and 72–100 (regarding exclusivist claims to salvation)).

32. Here, I do not wish to delve more deeply into the complex relationship between the a priori and the necessary (for a discussion of this relationship, see e.g. Quine, *Word*, 66–67). Here, I mean by 'necessary' simply 'independently of contingent factors'.

33. Examples of those conditions are that I know that I can usually trust my judgment on colors (say, I know that I am not color-blind and that my judgment on colors usually matches that of other people) and/or have reasons to doubt my discussion-partner's judgment (say, she often confuses red with green).

34. I distinguish the 'crude naturalism' of Dawkins and Co. from more sophisticated sorts. In a sense, I consider myself to be a naturalist: Given a distinction between methodological and ontological naturalism and a thorough reflection on the limits of the former, I endorse a methodological naturalism (see Grube, "Natur und Wissenschaft," 242–247). Yet, I do not wish to have this sort of naturalism in any way associated with the unreflective and crude naturalism Dawkins and Co. favor.

35. For this term, see another New Atheist, Dennett, *Spell*, 21.

36. I use the term 'scientific' in parentheses because I think that Dawkins and Co. use the notion of evidence in a spectacularly *un*scientific fashion: Their reference to evidence is ignorant of the current discussion in epistemology on evidence and the complexities it raises. One of those complexities is the question how much (of what kind of) evidence suffices to hold beliefs in a responsible fashion. Some commentators suggest that the answer to the question is dependent upon the pragmatic circumstances (see e.g. Fantl and McGrath, "Evidence Pragmatics," 67–94). Yet, if this were so, the term 'evidence' would have to be used in a very different fashion than is the case since the times of Clifford and Russell. However, Dawkins and Co. do not only use it in this (outdated) fashion but are unaware of the current discussion on it. Such a naivety is the opposite of a scientific attitude in my view.

37. Dawkin's *The God Delusion*, 272–278. Treatment of Stalin and Hitler – he conveniently overlooks other of his atheist 'bed-fellows' (to use his term), such as Pol Pot – is a master case of re-writing history: Hitler – i.e. the person who tried to eradicate (!) the Catholic Church in certain areas – is turned into a 'good Catholic'. I guess if you are among the 'brights', you do not have to worry about historical accuracy any longer…

38. Dawkins, *The God Delusion*, 329.

39. See ibid.

40. The Amish oppose only *the last two years* of school education, not school education as such. As Nussbaum (*Intolerance*, 127) has made clear, the Amish would have in all likelihood not have gotten away with preventing their children from going to school at all.

41. Historically, the main reason for allowing the Amish to have it their way was the way in which the distinction between public and private functions in the United States: This distinction implies, (a) that religion is not a public but a private affair and, (b) that the state should not interfere with private affairs. *This* is the main reason why the state does not interfere with Amish practices, such as this one, rather than the desire to enrich cultural diversity.

42. In order not to appear to be too naïve to Continental eyes, I would like to emphasize that I am aware of the extent to which cognition is construed rather than 'objectively given'. I have reconstructed and *endorsed* Thomas Kuhn's views on the incommensurability of paradigms as an insistence on the *irreducible subjectivity* of cognition (see Grube, "Interpreting Kuhn's Incommensurability-Thesis," 388–390). Yet, even if there is no such thing as 'objectively given' cognition, it would be highly counterintuitive to deny the differences between examples as that of the traffic light and more contested forms of cognition.

43. I have sketched such a route elsewhere, viz. in "Margolis' Critique of Bivalence," 252–257.
44. Van den Brom is 'amazed' about my switch from reflecting on bivalence to reflecting on justification. He considers it to be a 'change of subject'. I can understand the amazement since it would be more 'natural' to remain on the level of logics only. But I do not think that it is a change of subjects. Rather, I think that switching from bivalent truth to justification is a *further development*: In the face of the impasses into which insistence on a bivalent logic leads us, it is one among a variety of ways to pursue the issue of alterity in a promising fashion.
45. See Wolterstorff, "Obligation, Entitlement," 326–338 and 342–343 as well as Wolterstorff, *Practices of Beliefs*, 86–117 and 313–333.
46. Rorty, *Truth*, 2.
47. Stout, *Democracy*, 231; see also Stout, *Ethics*, 86 et al.
48. Jonathan Kvanvig, "Propositionalism", 10 (against Zagzebki's attempts to idealize the circumstances under which agents acquire beliefs).
49. Ibid. (Kvanvig quotes from Feldman).
50. Ibid. (emphasis mine).
51. Except that I have provided examples of obviously illegitimate or false beliefs, such as that of the color-blind person or the racist (see section 8).
52. 'Responsible' excludes postmodernist proposals which celebrate unrestrained diversity but would lead, if taken seriously, to a relativism or other disastrous consequences.
53. This is why I have recently defended Schwöbel's emphasis of the need to delve into the religious inside-perspectives over against the Enlightenment drive to focus on that which all religions have in common (see my "Schwöbels Thesen").
54. See Grube, "Willam James and Apologetics" and Grube, "Reconceptualizing Evidentialism".
55. A number of other conditions have to obtain as well, e.g. the absence of (overwhelming) evidence to the contrary and the context in which the belief is held must be a 'forced option' (see my reconstruction in "Apologetics", 313–315).
56. The situation may be different if internalism is coupled with idealizations (of the context in which the agent acquires her beliefs). Yet, the issue of idealization is a difficult one and invites a number of follow-up problems (see Kvanvig's criticism of Zagzebski above, section 9).
57. See, e.g. Roser/Seidel, *Ethik des Klimawandels*, 9. The issue is obviously very important when considering what (international) measures are to be taken against this exhaustion and what economic price we are willing to pay for taking these measures.
58. Obviously, these are all *prima facie* considerations. If I learn that the person holding D is on the payroll of, e.g. a coal-mining company, I will change my attitude and assume that she *is* biased.
59. What I call here 'reflecting on my own position (more thoroughly)' is related to what I called above, in the context of religious differences, as 'mirroring' my own religious beliefs in light of deviant religious beliefs.

## Bibliography

Albert, H. *Traktat über kritische Vernunft*. Tübingen: Mohr, 1980.
Dawkins, R. *The God Delusion*. London, Sydney: Transworld Publishers, 2006.
Dennett, D. *Breaking the Spell: Religion as a Natural Phenomenon*. London: Allen Lane, 2006.
Dummett, M. *Truth and Other Enigmas*. Cambridge, MA: Harvard University Press, 1978.
Everitt, N. "The Non-Existence of God." In *Reading Philosophy of Religion*, edited by G. Oppy and M. Scott, 127–132. Malden, MA: Wiley-Blackwell, 2010 (re-print).

Fantl, J., and M. McGrath. "Evidence, Pragmatics and Justification." *The Philosophical Review* 111, no. 1, January (2002): 67–94. doi:10.1215/00318108-111-1-67.

Flew, A. *God, Freedom, and Immortality.* New York, NY: Prometheus Books, 1984.

Goodman, N. *Ways of Worldmaking.* Indianapolis, IN: Hacket, 1978.

Grube, D.-M. "Alvin Plantingas Apologie des Glaubens." *Theologische Literaturzeitung* 139, no. 9 (2014): 965–982.

Grube, D.-M. "Empirisme, Postmodernisme en Godsdienstwijsbegeerte. De postmoderne kritiek op het empiristische denken en de consequenties voor de godsdienstwijsbegeerte." *Nederlands Theologisch Tijdschrift* 57 (2003): 321–337.

Grube, D.-M. "Interpreting Kuhn's Incommensurability-Thesis: Its Different Meanings and Epistemological Consequences." *Philosophy Study* 3, no. 5 (2013): 377–397.

Grube, D.-M. "Introduction." In *Pragmatism, Metaphysics and Culture: Reflections on the Philosophy of Joseph Margolis,* edited by D.-M. Grube and R. Sinclair, vi–xxvi. Helsinki: Nordic Studies in Pragmatism, 2015.

Grube, D.-M. "Margolis' Critique of Bivalence and its Consequences for the Theory of Action and a Pluralist Theory of Religion." In *Pragmatism, Metaphysics and Culture. Reflections on the Philosophy of Joseph Margolis,* edited by D.-M. Grube and R. Sinclair, 236–259. Helsinki: Nordic Studies in Pragmatism, 2015. http://www.nordprag.org/nsp/2/

Grube, D.-M. "Natur und Wissenschaft: Die Wissenschaftsauffassung im (kognitiven und ethischen) Naturalismus, in der anglo-amerikanischen Wissenschaftstheorie und in der gegenwärtigen Diskussion um die Evolutionstheorie (Dawkins)." In *Was heißt Natur? Philosophischer Ort und Begründungsfunktion des Naturbegriffs,* edited by E. Gräb-Schmidt, 241–276. Leipzig: Evangelische Verlagsanstalt, 2015.

Grube, D.-M. "Reconceptualizing Evidentialism and the Evidentialist Critique of Religion." In *William James on Religion,* edited by H. Rydenfelt and S. Pihlström, 145–164. New York, NY: Palgrave MacMillan, 2013.

Grube, D.-M. "Schwöbels Thesen zum religiösen Pluralismus und seine Kritik an John Hick." *"Festschrift" for Christoph Schwöbel's 60th Birthday,* edited by M. Mühling, D.-M. Grube, et al. 289–302. Göttingen: Vandenhoeck & Ruprecht, forthcoming.

Grube, D.-M. "Willam James and Apologetics. Why 'The Will to Believe' Argument Succeeds." *Neue Zeitschrift für Systematische Theologie und Religionsphilosophie* 46 (2004): 306–329.

King, P. *Toleration.* London: Allen and Unwin, 1976.

Kvanvig, J. "Propositionalism and the Perspectival Character of Justification." *American Philosophical Quarterly* 40, no. 1 (2003): 3–16.

Margolis, J. *Pragmatism without Foundations: Reconciling Realism and Relativism.* Oxford, New York: Blackwell, 1986.

Margolis, J. *The Truth about Relativism.* Oxford UK: Blackwell, 1991.

Margolis, J. *Historied Thought, Constructed World. A Conceptual Primer for the Turn of the Millennium.* Berkeley, Los Angeles, London: University of California Press, 1995.

McKim, R. *On Religious Diversity.* Oxford, New York: Oxford University Press, 2012.

Nussbaum, M. *The New Religious Intolerance.* Cambridge, MA, London: Harvard University Press, 2012.

Plantinga, A. *Warranted Christian Belief.* Oxford, New York: Oxford University Press, 2000.

Quine, W. V. O. *Word and Object.* Cambridge, MA: The MIT Press, 1960.

Rorty, R. *Philosophy and the Mirror of Nature.* Princeton: Princeton University Press, 1979.

Rorty, R. "Is there a Problem about Fictional Discourse?" In *Consequences of Pragmatism,* edited by R. Rorty, 110–138. Minneapolis: University of Minnesota Press, 1982.

Rorty, R. *Truth and Progress. Philosophical Papers.* Volume 3. Cambridge: Cambridge University Press, 1998.

Roser, D, and C. Seidel, eds. *Ethik des Klimawandels. Eine Einführung.* Darmstadt: Wissenschaftliche Buchgesellschaft, 2013.

Russell, B. "On Denoting." *Mind* 14, no. 56 October (1905): 485–493.

Stout, J. *Ethics after Babel. The Languages of Morals and Their Discontents.* Boston: Beacon Press, 1988.

Stout, J. *Democracy and Tradition.* Princeton: Princeton University Press, 2004.

Tillich, P. "The Two Types of Philosophy of Religion." *Main Works/Hauptwerke,* 4 vols. edited by J. Clayton, 289–300. Berlin, New York: De Gruyter, 1987.

Trigg, R. *Religious Diversity. Philosophical and Political Implications*. New York, NY: Cambridge University Press, 2014.

Wolterstorff, N. "Obligation, Entitlement, and Rationality." In *Contemporary Debates in Epistemology*, edited by M. Steup and E. Sosa, 326–338, 342–343. Malden, Oxford, Carlton: Blackwell, 2005.

Wolterstorff, Nicholas. *Practices of Beliefs. Selected Essays*, II vol. Terence Cuneo et al. edited by Cambridge, New York: Cambridge University Press, 2010.

# Index

Note: Page numbers followed by 'n' refer to notes

INDEX

For Product Safety Concerns and Information please contact our EU
representative GPSR@taylorandfrancis.com Taylor & Francis Verlag GmbH,
Kaufingerstraße 24, 80331 München, Germany


Printed and bound by CPI Group (UK) Ltd, Croydon, CR0 4YY
08/06/2025
01896999-0016